[S]elections in Minnesota: An Introduction to How Machines Controlled 2020

And Why We Must Return to Hand Counting Paper Ballots

Erik van Mechelen

[S]elections in Minnesota: An Introduction to How Machines Controlled 2020

And Why We Must Return to Hand Counting Paper Ballots

Erik van Mechelen

ISBN 979-8-218-02893-0

© 2022 Erik van Mechelen

To every soul patiently enduring the present trials and who with active persistence are running the race presented to them.

Contents

Introduction - A Totalitarian Flavor 1
    Control Through Machines 18

Chapter One - Preparation 29
    Minnesota Statutes and Election Law 33
    Modern Electronic Election Systems 35
    The Statewide Voter Registration System (SVRS) 37
    Epollbooks 42
    Ballot Preparation 45
    Voting Machines 47
    Tabulation Systems 57
    Influence Operations 60

Chapter Two - Attack 63
    Did Ballot Traffickers Work in Minnesota? 65

Chapter Three - Backup Attack 71
    Edison Zero 72
    Rhode Island 74
    Minnesota's Simulation 81

Chapter Four - Defense 91
    Part of Their Plan? 92
    700,000 Reported Absentee Voters Not Connected in SVRS 94
    Minnesota Post Election Review Reveals Missing Ballots 95
    A Petition to Stop the Certification of Minnesota's Election 97

CONTENTS

    Crow Wing County 99
    Dakota County 103
    Wright County 104
    Morrison County 105
    Sherburne County 105
    Where Are the Cast Vote Records? 106
    Pushing Back Against Tyranny 113
    Then vs. Now 116

Chapter Five - Minnesota in 2022 119
    The Preparation Phase in Minnesota for 2022 122
    MNGOP Pressures Republicans 123
    Confirmed and Documented Tampering of Delegate Lists 128
    Endorsing Conventions 135
    The Secretary of State Endorsement 139
    How Much is a Party Endorsement Worth? 154
    Electronic Voting 156
    Primary Election on August 9 159

Chapter Six - Recommendations 161
    Small Counties with Great Potential 163
    Objections to Hand Counting 164
    How Much Do Machine Elections Cost? 165
    The County Commission Strategy 169
    Resolutions 170
    Are You a County Commissioner, City Council Member,
        or Township Supervisor? 172
    Are You a Candidate? 175
    Use Your Platform 176
    Do You Have A Few Minutes Per Day? 177
    Vote in Person in the Primary and Midterm Elections . . 178

Chapter Seven - Security Threats to Our Election System 181
    Election Infrastructure Components 181
    Consequences of Election Infrastructure Security Breaches 187

Chapter Eight - Where We Go From Here 193
    What Diplomacy Teaches 195
    The Power of Information 198

Chapter Nine - A Brief History of Voting Machines and
    Certifications 201
    Putting the History in Context 208
    Certifications Are Less Than Useless 209

Afterward 219

Introduction - A Totalitarian Flavor

"There's no way we can ever trust a computer system built with components made overseas, particularly in China, or assembled in China, let alone both, and that's what we have in our voting system, unfortunately."

—Col. Shawn Smith, USAF, Ret. – 25 year Air Force veteran and the former director and test manager for the operational testing of complex, computer-based weapon systems and a subject matter expert on the security of computer-based election systems, calling into a Tarrant County, Texas meeting[1]

---

[1] https://rumble.com/v15st7w-military-cyber-security-expert-why-no-county-should-use-electronic-voting-s.html

Dominion, Made in China

2005 – Beijing, China

As the two buses converged from the left and right into our lane I wondered whether this road was safe for bicycles. When we'd agreed to tea fifteen minutes prior my family wasn't expecting to navigate a minor highway on two wheels. Our tour guide slipped through the gap, not far behind were Mom and Dad who decided to go for it. My brothers and I were forced to brake and cars behind us honked, not in solidarity, but at least they didn't hit us. Losing sight of Mom and Dad as the buses zipped the lane shut, I briefly imagined them being crushed. Moments later, materializing out of the cloud of exhaust on that hazy winter morning were Mom and Dad and the guide, each still in their saddle. It was 2005 and there were far fewer bikes and many more motorized vehicles in Beijing than I'd recalled in our 1998 visit. That year, just before the people's uprising in Jakarta prompted Suharto to step aside from the Indonesian Presidency after a thirty-two-year reign, on one day's notice we flew into Singapore; after receiving word that school was canceled for the year, we decided to visit China.

Seven years later, biking through China's capital city, we navigated the tight alleys, connecting traditional courtyard residences in Old Beijing, some dating back to the thirteenth century. Parking next to a red door beneath a slanting tiled roof, our guide knocked and announced us. A smiling, elderly woman with wise wrinkles answered and soon we stepped over the threshold and were shown to a small room adjacent the courtyard. Without heating we did not take off our coats, but here at least the walls sheltered us from the wind's bite. We were all keen for the hot tea soon set before us but especially thankful was my older brother whose frozen hands around the cup were eventually thawed, albeit painfully. We sat around a low stone table and sipped our tea while our guide translated the woman's story, her family's history, and what life was like in her community folded into the heart of the city.

Having expended considerable physical effort and survived both the elements and highway traffic, we were as travelers taking temporary refuge from a storm, content for simple pleasures. We were soon transported through time by our host's tale.

After receiving my high school diploma from the International School of Beijing in 2006, I soon returned to the United States to attend college in Minnesota. In short order however I learned that back in the Chinese capital several thousand traditional homes just like the one we'd visited, along with their more than seven hundred years of history, were bulldozed. Ostensibly this was done to make room for sports venues and other infrastructure for the 2008 Olympic Games, but word on the street was that the Party was embarrassed by the hutong, which were downtrodden and often occupied by the poor. I learned that the residents at the time of their evictions were not compensated appropriately to the point that they couldn't easily find other places to live.

My family had lived in Shunyi District, a rural area east of Beijing. The street between our school and the local villages was still covered in autumn by corn kernels laid to dry by farmers. In their communities my new school friends once treated me to tasty and filling noon meal for about a dollar a person.

Corn Drying on Road

It was not clear how long these rural areas would last as the city expanded eastward toward us. I remember large clusters of residential apartment buildings rising quickly from the landscape, one day webbed by bamboo scaffolding, completed the next. To this day I wonder how many of the workers who toiled all day and through the night were not Chinese but North Korean workers on surreptitious loan. The pace of building in the last decade contributed to the ghost city phenomenon; the sociological manifestation of a "one child" policy the Chinese ruling class boasted of—as the rest of the world shrugged its shoulders and my home country stood side by side with China and North Korea in its late-stage abortion stance. While my two brothers and I sat in a tea shop near the Terra Cotta warriors museum in Xi'an, a plate of melon arrived without our request, the server softly murmuring "san ge xiong di" (three brothers) as she faded away.

Prior to our arrival I knew little about China. When I shared with my history teacher in Houston, Texas that my family was moving to Beijing, he remarked, raising his eyebrows, "That's interesting... you know, China is a Communist country." Actually, I didn't *really* know what that meant. I thought the term merely referred to an economic system, a contrast to capitalism. At age seventeen without the context of Communist disasters throughout Earth's recent history, I was going in blind.

It would take years for my eyes to be truly opened about Communism. But my first glimpses of understanding came in the usual ways: exploring my surroundings, through conversations, in books. With my adventurous mother I walked the wild unrestored sections of the Great Wall and glimpsed how the people lived in the villages nestled against the ancient divider visible from space. On my return in 2008, in broken Chinese I chatted with migrant workers outside the gates of East China Normal University in Shanghai while they cooked delicious dumplings or slapped dough on the inside of a metal barrel. The bread man travelled daily from outside the sprawling city, here standing all day in the cold and sometimes rain competing with other sellers to sell portions for a one or two yuan (25 cents) a piece. I came to learn through my classmate Deanna's research that he was one of approximately 300 million migrant workers throughout the country, at the time equivalent to the entire population of the United States. The international press lauded the country's economic growth but there was a tragic number of people yet to rise out of poverty. Maybe one day those people will be liberated from their totalitarian government, just as we here in the United States must liberate ourselves, reclaiming our government from the failed and corrupt political establishment.

The early 2000s was rough on the people of China, but the near-term past was arguably tougher. Mao's policies devastated the country and as a result tens of millions of lives were lost. The chaperone of the 2008 trip, an economics professor who grew up during the Cultural Revolution, shared with me how she and her grandmother hid in the kitchen stove when Mao's Red Guards showed up unannounced and took her father away, never to be seen again. In Ji Xianlin's *The Cowshed: Memories of the Chinese Cultural Revolution*[2], I learned how a once-respected professor was interrogated by his own students and made to build a holding cell for he and fellow intellectual colleagues labeled class enemies. These were commonplace experiences, normalizing total control of the mind and body for what no one in their right mind (not even Mao) would truly suffer. The total control of the Chinese population was first instantiated in fear, then through elections, establishing a uniparty governance model since the foundation of the Chinese Communist Party (CCP) in 1949.

While I didn't have a robust understanding of the comparative political models in question nor their sinister underpinnings (that go well beyond mere politics), I knew that when I left China it wasn't a place I would ever want to live for very long. Evenings walking our neighborhood I wondered whether the guards were there for our safety or as our monitors—at least they were friendly, a reminder that many even today are good people just doing their jobs. In our living room below two fire alarms—the purpose of the second my family never did surmise—the television regularly went static at any mention of China. Our church services were held in a conference room since there were no churches and Chinese nationals were forbidden from attending.

When I moved back to the United States of America I had a deeper appreciation for the spirit of freedom, central to our founding and identity. But I have come to understand there is a veneer that when peeled back reveals layer upon layer of deceptions to be first understood and then confronted. When I was renting a car to drive to the MNGOP state convention in Rochester, Minnesota, the man renting me the car, a businessman from Tanzania, described

[2]https://www.amazon.com/Cowshed-Memories-Chinese-Cultural-Revolution/dp/1590179269

commonplace corruption in his country of origin. He went on to say, "In America corruption is hidden with fancy names."

As rumors of mysterious virus spread in early 2020, I immediately sensed a contest of ideas was about to play out. I remembered SARS-CoV-1 from my childhood in Asia; this felt different. An attempt at total control was being instantiated with fear not only in the United States but globally. Little did I know that a system-altering election would follow. Before he became President Trump, on October 23, 2016 the 45th President said[3], "This is not simply another four-year election. This is a crossroads in the history of our civilization that will determine whether or not We The People reclaim control over *our* government." And when the deeply corrupt are confronted, it is to be expected that like cornered prey they will fight and fight dirty to prevent their corruption from coming into the light.

By mid-summer of 2020, videos documenting the horrors of the Chinese Cultural Revolution were circulating on YouTube. After several weeks of violence plaguing cities around the United States, loudly—though in substance quite loosely—tethered to the death of several United States citizens who the corporate media branded as victims. The corporate sponsored revolutionaries used the color of these citizen's skin as justification for their looting, pillaging, assaulting, and killing. The corporate media and intellectual class graced these actors with the blessed heritage of "peaceful" protest, as small businesses were destroyed, communities (many of them populated by racial and ethnic minorities) gutted, and cities burned. Law enforcement largely stood down. No one seemed to bother to check the police reports. Why would they? Instagram and Facebook already told them what happened, and whose name (no matter how criminal, felonious, or murderous) to say. The same tactics the Maoist used in the previous century to upend China were on display in my home country—tearing down statues, disgracing public buildings, ridiculing our history, shaming any who would defend it. Where the American version of the red army (the black

---

[3] https://www.facebook.com/watch/?v=10157885740135725

shirts) stopped short was public beheadings—perhaps knowing that the constitutional right to bear arms and form militias would put a swift end to what could be accomplished with a more measured and insidious approach.

Living in Minneapolis, the totalitarian flavor of the air, food, and water I remembered in Beijing was asserting itself in my own backyard.

After months of isolation, fear, confusion, anxiety, and frustration, with (major sporting leagues around the world shut down) nothing to watch and nowhere to go, a series of provocative images from the corner of 38th and Chicago in Minneapolis's Powderhorn neighborhood lit a powder keg. The nation, within moments, went from "stronger together" to irredeemably and systemically racist. With half-truth history populating the minds of the highly educated and the pages of the New York Times, the Maoist attempt at unraveling of the American consciousness was now out in the open. Minneapolis would be center stage of the supposedly anti-fascist to deliver their first blow to the supposedly white supremacist fabric of our nation's past, present, and future. Soon, the epicenter of the charade would ripple out to its final landing place (for the moment) in Portland where the (apparently well-funded) black shirts terrorized a city ironically praised for its leftist ideals. But while the nightly news celebrated the "mostly peaceful" protests that were plainly seen as nothing of the sort, a more profound war was raging across the country in state houses of government and county elections commissions...

From Patrick Colbeck's *The 2020 Coup: What Happened. What We Can Do.*, the preparation phase, where weaknesses are widened and new ones are created, was well under way. The elections commissions, the non-profits, the state legislatures, judicial permissions, and corporate media swirled in a whirlwind of confusion that unconstitutionally set the election to the tune they wanted to play.

Dr. Shiva, MIT PhD and inventor of email, with Mike Lindell nearby

By the next summer (2021), I was working with men and women around the state searching for a way to properly and seriously audit Minnesota's election results and materials, including the machines. Being part of that group was short lived (it was infiltrated) but that work got me into to the Cyber Symposium in August. That week in Sioux Falls, South Dakota helped me better understand what was at stake. The PCAPs may not have been legit, but Mesa County Clerk Tina Peters, flown to South Dakota by Mike Lindell, *is*. I still had much to learn, and still do.

Shortly after, I joined a decentralized national working group facilitated by a former refugee from the Communist regime in Vietnam named Hoang Quan, a friend of David and Erin Clements (who delivered the Otero County and Torrance County presentation[4], arguably the best examples in county commission settings as part of their audits of about nine New Mexico counties which even the Congressional Oversight Committee in Washington D.C. tried to shut down. On Thursday, June 9, 2022, their dedication led

---

[4] https://rumble.com/v16cc09-torrance-county-commission-estancia-new-mexico-may-25-2022.html

to Otero County, New Mexico county commissioners voting to remove Zuckerberg drop boxes and Dominion Voting machines and other election machines for the midterm election in a unanimous decision.

Otero County, New Mexcio followed only Nye County, Nevada, and Esmeralda County, Nevada in making a move *away* from machines, joining only a handful of counties and townships[5] nationwide which hand count paper ballots.

Days later the Otero County commissioners refused to certify their June 7, 2022 primary, in part because of Dominion Voting Systems' noncompliance with the New Mexico election code, a move which perhaps signals the beginning of a "lesser magistrates" trend to finally end tyrannical overreach.

From the outset, the working group's focus was uncovering the truth about elections state by state, county by county, as well as providing a place where information could be shared about the January 6 prisoners, arguably the first prisoners of war in the battle to expose the coup of November 3rd. This documentary on January 6[6] and others like it makes the treatment of those prisoners even more heartless. Audio recordings like this one from Jeremy Brown[7] on June 8, 2022 (on the 253rd day of his illegal, unconstitutional imprisonment) show you the character and resolve of those prisoners of war.

Our communication largely took place on Telegram. People gathered from across the country; stories could be written about each. Some had gone to work *before* the 2020 elections or had covered elections for years or decades: data analysts, engineers, and researchers were among them, as well as those who knew in their hearts something was very wrong about November 3, 2020. What

---
[5] https://electioninvestigationlaw.org/county-status/
[6] https://www.thegatewaypundit.com/2022/06/exclusive-truth-january-6th-documentary-premieres-today-gateway-pundit-narrated-political-prisoner-jake-lang-inside-solitary-confinement-must-watch/
[7] https://www.dropbox.com/s/t1cd039l5bguf7f/Jeremy68call.mp3?dl=0

all of us had in common was a dedication to carrying the burden of Truth.

Perhaps many of these men and women won't get formal recognition for their sacrifices, but part of my aim in this short book is to provide a window into the work they were doing and continue doing to help the rest of us understand what happened and how we can fix it. Despite two years as a software analyst at Target, it was apparent early on that I did not always follow the technical details of discussions. But in understanding *just enough* the door was opened for me to translate to non-technical people the core of the machine-related issues.

The links and resources sprinkled throughout this book represent dozens if not hundreds of hours of content synthesized from hundreds or thousands of hours of work from various individuals, and probably millions of hours in total if one aggregates the work of people across the country since November 3rd, 2020. I for one am extremely grateful for the sacrifices so many have made and for those sacrifices they continue to make.

Jeffrey O'Donnell, a data analyst, was among those I sat in a couple virtual meetings with around September 2021, who in April 2022 shared the following:

"Not since the Manhattan Project, which developed the Atom Bomb, have so many smart people worked together to solve such a critical problem. We have hard evidence now of ballot manipulation in the Mesa County database, and this is serving as a "Rosetta Stone" allowing us to find the same "fingerprints" in other counties. Vote records and Voter Rolls have been acquired from dozens of states and counties all over the country, and myriad phantom voters have been identified. The existence of paid "ballot mules" is now a proven fact[8]. Every method of attack we identify and publish can be prevented, mitigated, or at the very least quickly identified in the next election."

---

[8] https://rumble.com/v169mjd-yes-sir.html

In early 2022 I supported local teams forming in about a dozen Minnesota counties benefitting from Rick Weible's data, strategic thinking, and leadership. My role was mostly to bring my video camera to county commissioner meetings, workshops, or closed door meetings in Dakota, Sherburne, Wright, and Morrison County. (I've spoken in Sherburne County[9] and also recorded open comments in my home county of Hennepin, which still conducts virtual meetings.) I listened, asked questions, and learned. These interactions confirmed many concerns I had from reviewing the data and convinced me change was needed.

Even if we are not yet aware of an exhaustive list of machine manipulation, there is more than enough to understand that the machines must be turned off. Too many known vulnerabilities; too many unknowns remain.

The responses of the secretaries of state around the country has largely been defensive. There is not yet enough sense of urgency from election officials nor county commissioners. Freedom of information act (FOIA) requests and public data requests too often lead to unsatisfying answers. In the future, however, the foundation of public information available promptly to the public will set the tone for civic engagement and public accountability. We cannot give up on this vision.

A return to hand counting paper ballots is probably the only safe near term solution to restore confidence in elections. Of course people can still try to cheat and will try. But at least then we won't have both computers and people cheating. The near term goal is to reduce and minimize fraud.

To this end, county elections must be retaken to reestablish local control and oversight. The citizens of, say, Todd County, MN may not have confidence with the results in neighboring Morrison County, but if they removed machines and voted Amish (and many people in Todd County are Amish), then at least they might have

---

[9]https://youtu.be/gKZjZMFlj8w

confidence in the results of local races. County commissioners are starting to realize and manifest their power to refuse to certify local elections which they and their constituents cannot trust on account of them being run on equipment that breaks state election codes.

Through work toward audits, reporting on the work of others, and attending county commissioner meetings, I've met Minnesotans from all walks of life, each fighting for their state and ultimately their lives and their children's futures through a dedication to the truth. Too many to name, so here are just a few:

People like Rick Weible[10], founder of D3Defense[11], whose database analysis of the statewide voter registration system (SVRS) highlighted that there were more than 700,000 absentee voters reported than documented in the SVRS five days *after* the MN Canvassing Board certified the election. People like Teri Dickinson who has worked tirelessly arranging and promoting Rick's events and activating others in her community. People like Susan Shogren Smith[12] who filed a petition[13](Case Number A20-1486) to correct errors and omissions under Minnesota Statute §204B.44[14] before the MN State Canvassing Board certified the election on Tuesday, November 24, 2022. People like Edwin Hahn[15] who was one of only seven people in Minnesota to file an election contest for the 2020 election that went all the way to the Supreme Court. People like Jeremy Pekula[16] who helped to bring Captain Seth Keshel[17] to the Brainerd Exchange[18] (speaking alongside Rick Weible and Susan Smith), set up a meeting between us and his county commissioners and election officials, and is running to be the next Morrison County

---

[10] https://midwestswampwatch.com/
[11] https://www.d3defense.org/
[12] https://shogrensmithlaw.com/about-us
[13] https://img1.wsimg.com/blobby/go/47803963-5178-4387-9865-0ea08f5332bd/downloads/22%2005%2006%202020%20attachments%20with%20cover%20page.pdf?ver=1653579701201
[14] https://www.revisor.mn.gov/statutes/cite/204B.44
[15] https://wewinwithedwin.com
[16] https://www.facebook.com/PekulaForThePeople/
[17] https://captk.com/
[18] https://erikvanmechelen.substack.com/p/motion-passed-to-request-minnesota

Commissioner in District 3. People like Kari Watkins[19] running for county commissioner in Sherburne County. People like Pastor Ben Davis[20], also running for office as a state representative, who spoke at multiple county commissioner meetings in Crow Wing County leading to the commissioners voting 4-1 to ask Secretary of State Steve Simon to do an audit of Crow Wing County's 2020 election, which was declined[21]. People like Kim Bauer[22] who did not stand down after it appeared her school board election in 2021 was stolen from her in ISD 196—still unresolved more than half a year later despite multiple meetings with county election officials in Dakota County. And people like Robin Sylvester[23] who helped to organize a door-to-door and digital canvas of parts of 30 Minnesota counties, also running for Crow Wing County Board. There are many more who deserve credit and some of their work will be included in the pages that follow.

In mid-to-late April 2022 I decided to run for secretary of state in Minnesota and made the announcement on May 3rd[24] standing on the back of a pickup truck before joining patriots urging their Sherburne County commissioners to have a public hearing about their electronic voting systems. Why am I doing this? To continue sharing what I've learned about what happened in 2020 and how we can heal our sick election system.

At the time the decision felt partially absurd. What good would it do to run in a system that was unfair and lacked transparency? I thought to myself, *They will probably just rig it against me*. In my childhood I saw millions go to the streets in Jakarta, Indonesia which influenced the then three-decade president Suharto to resign. And yet this is a different place and time. We can do this by the book. That "book" now includes concepts like the "lesser magistrates"—an

---

[19] https://www.youtube.com/watch?v=IFlEhMwqowg
[20] https://www.bendavismn.com/
[21] https://erikvanmechelen.substack.com/p/steve-simon-fears-disinformation
[22] https://www.hometownsource.com/sun_thisweek/free/district-196-school-board-candidate-kim-bauer/article_15d5b88e-062f-11ec-a902-e35a9e0131e3.html
[23] https://www.robinford2.com/
[24] https://rumble.com/v13i4tm-mn-secretary-of-state-announcement.html

output of which can be seen in county commissioners exercising their power to refuse to certify local elections.

In the Recommendations chapter you will find detailed steps every Minnesota county can take *right now*. We cannot afford to wait for the primary or the general election to make changes happen. By then, our county commissioners should be well aware of their powers and the expectations their constituents have of them.

As uneasy as I felt about running for secretary of state in Minnesota, I was also eager to take the opportunity set before me. If I hadn't decided to run, a few things would not have happened:

1. I wouldn't have been excluded without a satisfying reason by the MNGOP from the secretary of state endorsement process at the Rochester state convention on May 12 and 13, 2022, nor learned that others are being pressured not to speak with me or invite me to events
2. I wouldn't be writing this short free book (or recording the audiobook)
3. In doing so, I wouldn't have learned as much as I have from writing it

If I've done my job well, readers will eagerly forward the PDF and .mp3 files of this book to their friends, family, and coworkers.

Everyone, even those who've shown less curiosity about whether our elections are fair or not. Forgive them for they know not what they do. Each of us has the right to know the truth in a timely manner. Without good information, it is harder to make decisions or take decisive impactful actions.

The decision to run for office has also has helped my overall approach. Where in the past I led with frustration and anger, now I seek solutions and aim to help everyone learn and improve while also holding everyone to a high standard. That goes for me, too. Like hiring managers interviewing candidates, those who may vote for me deserve to first see a body of work from the past year in particular. And if I do get to serve as the secretary of state, I want to have already built relationships with county-level election officials and commissioners who will rely on me to do my job and help them do theirs once in office. I want to show them how it is I work to get things done. This has already changed my interaction with election officials, whether in person or on the phone. And yet they should know that I will ask for excellence and also courage.

Previously I approached matters primarily from an investigative approach, but now I balance that mindset with an encouraging attitude which I believe will inspire change—change in hearts and then change in the process and system. There's another reason to adjust, which is based on conversations with many people inside and outside the election process. That is, in my opinion many election officials are still learning about the vulnerabilities in the suite of electronic voting equipment in use by their county's election process. After all, most county election officials are not cybersecurity experts. Few of us are in the wider populace, which makes discussion of much of this subject matter even trickier. Short of removing machines from the system, only a cybersecurity expert would understand how to mitigate the risks inherent in the modern electronic voting system.

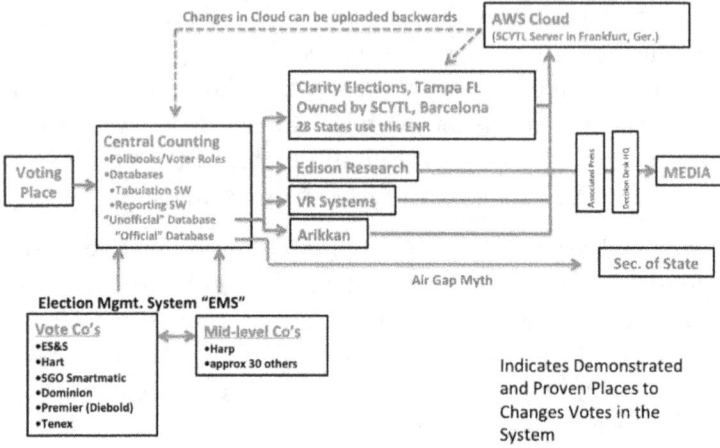

Very High Level View of Voting System, Networks and Attack Entry Points
There are no security standards, it's easy to change votes with no audit trail

Demonstrated and Proven Places to Changes Votes in the System

What we know, and what will be shown in documentaries like Selection Code[25], is that those who control the machines, control the results. So long as we have a complex modern electronic voting system coupled with restrictive audit-related election laws, I will not feel any confidence whatsoever that my vote was counted. Do you?

It is a major victory for the enemy if we were to make many reforms to our election process but still keep our current modern electronic voting system as is. Do not be fooled by concessions that distract you from the goal.

Control Through Machines

From the 100,000-foot view, elections are simply a control mechanism and also a critical vector of attack against a nation-state. Here in the United States, we arguably made this easier not only

---

[25] https://selectioncode.com

by allowing private entities like Dominion or ES&S or Hart Inter Civic to provide the majority of our electronic voting equipment but also by outsourcing some of the coding involved in that critical infrastructure to places like Serbia in the case of Dominion's source code as proven by the name of a Serbian developer found in the code.

Here in the United States, if by subverting elections you can routinely install candidates up and down the ballot, then a county, state, and country can over time be usurped without firing a bullet—very useful in a country where citizens are very well armed. In the digital age, this can be done through machine code invisible to election judges, poll challengers, and election officials. Meanwhile, the public (myself very much included) could be manipulated and poisoned for years or decades through government-run schools, social media, and especially intelligence-agency-designed influence operations to think all is well in our constitutional republic, when in fact we were on course to lose it and may indeed have lost it for good, unless we act decisively. Every attitude, intent, and action shapes the world we live in.

Of course, maintaining control by subverting elections is not new, even if this important fact is not widely understood.

In 2010, at the IEEE International Conference on Computing, Control and Industrial Engineering, in Wuhan, China, a paper was presented titled "Research on PID control parameters tuning based on Election-survey Optimization Algorithm"[26] which discusses improvements offered by the election-survey optimization algorithm (ESO) above and beyond the Ziegler-Nichols (Z-N) tuning method of 1942.

---

[26]https://ieeexplore.ieee.org/document/5492031

Introduction - A Totalitarian Flavor

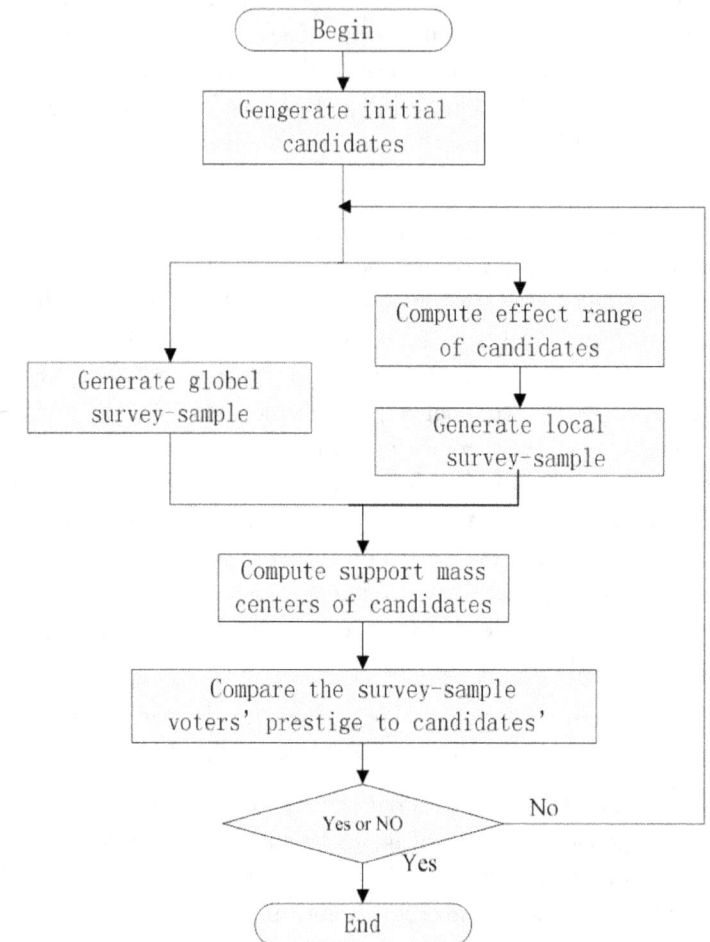

Fig.1 The flow chart of ESO Algorithm

The ESO algorithm

Proportional–Integral–Derivative (PID) controllers are used for many practical applications from tuning your house's temperature to the accurate production of cheese in a plant. Was a similar algorithm potentially used in the November 3, 2020 general election?

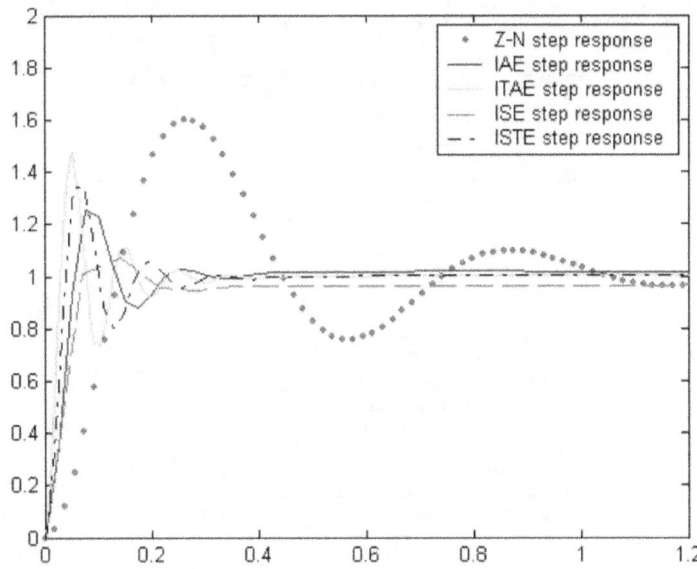

Fig.6 Step response of PID control with Z-N and optimal parameters

In Chapter Three - Backup Attack, the shape of this graph will be compared to Edison Research's election night reported results

In 2004, Sequoia (acquired the next year in 2005 by Smartmatic, which has software running on the latest Dominion, ES&S, and Hart machines), was used to run the Venezuelan presidential recall election[27], even though it was the company's first time providing machines for an election. Was this a test run of their hardware and software for future elections?

Before electronic voting machines, decades prior, we know that elections were a big business, as evidenced by this $20 million contract in 1973[28].

---

[27]https://maloney.house.gov/media-center/press-releases/smartmatic-announces-sale-sequoia-voting-systems
[28]https://projectapario.com/timeline/RR111FF911F18III444F

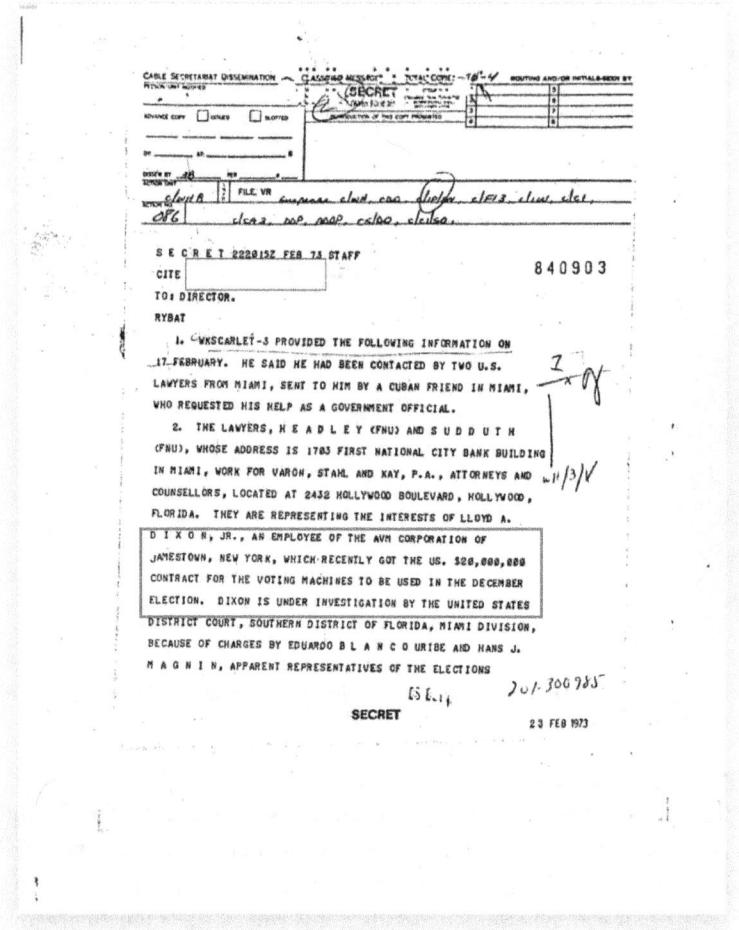

$20,000,000 contract in 1973

Twelve years prior, in 1961, this airtel to the Director of the FBI[29] I found while browsing the JFK files on Project Apario[30] suggests overt election subversion:

[29] https://projectapario.com/Browse?document=6BH3XSPCQ&from_search_query=stumble_into&filename=docid-32296189.pdf&from_page_identifier=BSJPPLS4T
[30] https://projectapario.com

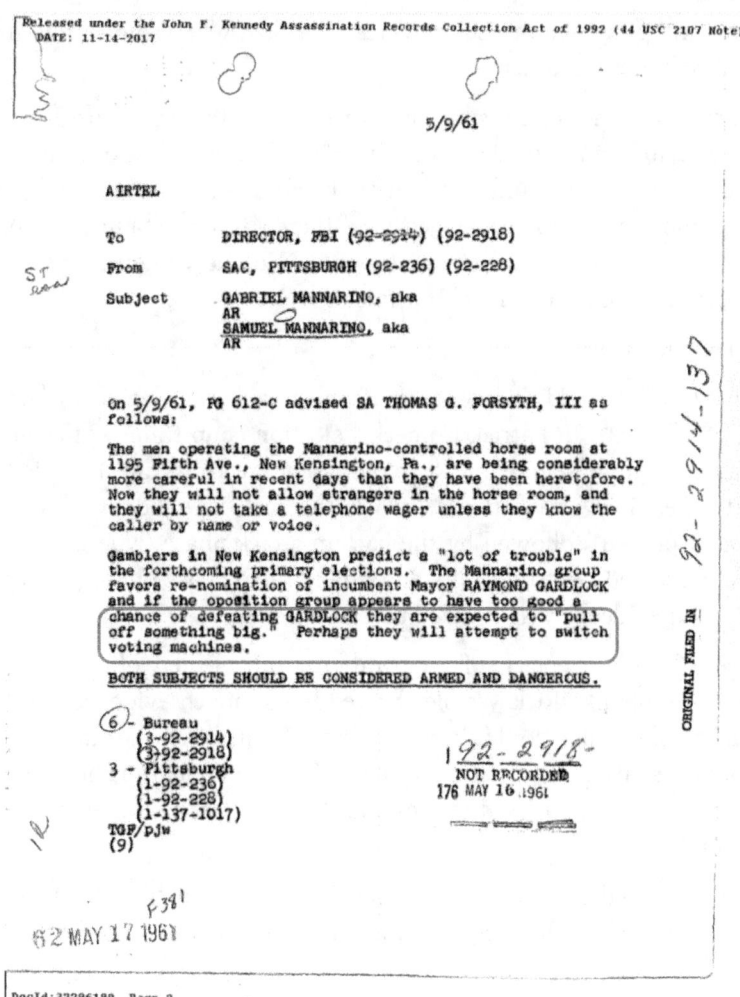

Perhaps they will attempt to switch voting machines

A dozen years earlier, in Robert A. Caro's autobiography, *Working*[31], Caro stresses the importance of facts being made available to the public. In 1948 at the eleventh hour two hundred votes were found for Lyndon B. Johnson propelling him into the Texas Senate

---

[31]https://www.amazon.com/Working-Robert-Caro/dp/0525656340

by a margin of eighty-seven votes in a race where more than a million votes were cast.

Caro found the man responsible for carrying this out, Luis Salas, who invited him into his home where he admitted to Caro what he did and that he lied under oath about it. He gave Caro a manuscript describing his actions. Caro writes, "Thanks to that manuscript, it would not be necessary for me to write, 'No one will ever be sure if Lyndon Johnson stole it.' He stole it."

That was in 1948.

Like Caro, I couldn't look away from what I was seeing in late 2020 and 2021. In Patrick Colbeck's election coup framework, the preparation phase (creating weaknesses in laws and rules) had led into the main attack phase (where the mail-in ballot weakness was exploited) followed by the backup attack phase (where votes were injected electronically), and finally the defense phase (where election evidence was covered up or destroyed).

Even despite the lack of cooperation from elected officials, locally people like Rick Weible showed me so much evidence from Minnesota that I couldn't stand aside. From others around the country sharing information with me, I gradually learned how our elections were supposed to work, and how in practice they could be undermined.

The election theft in 2020 was obviously coordinated. If exploitation like this has been happening for a long time, why only now was it so obvious?

How was it that I'd so far lived my life believing my vote counted, but now could not so easily answer that question? That will take some time to unpack, but based on the full frontal attack upon President Trump's character (and attempts on his life), it was clear from the enemy's perspective another four years of Trump could not be tolerated. So they threw the kitchen sink at him come election time. Would things have been better if Biden had not been allowed to be installed? Mike Lindell's opinion at the Cyber

Symposium was this: Thank God because otherwise we wouldn't know about the machines.

One thing is clear, from national Rasmussen polls[32] and conversations I've had personally: Since November 3, 2020, tens of millions of Americans, if not more, have asked or are now beginning to ask, Does my vote count? It's only a matter of time before that number goes north of 100 million and almost everyone curious to know the facts will have the chance to understand the sobering implications.

If our election officials, counties, and secretaries of state cannot show (19 months after November 3, 2020) that the computerized election management systems used to produce election results actually do so without error, then citizens in increasing numbers will continue to lose trust in the current system.

Jeffrey O'Donnell puts it well in the introduction to his Mesa County #3 Report[33], highlighted in the forthcoming [S]election Code documentary: "If Americans' votes are to be recorded and counted by machines, every aspect of those machines' operation, configuration, and data must be recorded, immediately available at no cost or administrative burden to citizens and their independent examiners and confirmed 100% accurate through that independent verification. The absence or shortfall of any of those three imperatives (recorded, available, and independently verified) should immediately cause the public to distrust both the purported results from those machines, and also anyone who insists that they accept those results."

This book will follow the organization of the four phases of an election coup put forward by Patrick Colbeck in *The 2020 Coup*[34],

---

[32] https://www.rasmussenreports.com/public_content/politics/general_politics/may_2022/election_integrity_most_voters_still_suspect_cheating
[33] https://magaraccoon.com/docs/MesaCountyReport3.pdf
[34] https://www.amazon.com/2020-Coup-What-Happened-Can/dp/1955043655/

currently the best book on this topic (and excerpted at the end of this one):

1. **Preparation** - create weaknesses and shape the landscape through laws, procedures, rules, electronic systems, and influence operations
2. **Main Attack** - exploit the greatest weakness, absentee and mail-in ballots
3. **Backup Attack** - execute contingency plans such as injecting votes digitally
4. **Defense** - cover up or destroy evidence of the main attack and backup attack

These phases will provide the framework to put Minnesota's 2020 election in context.

In the imminent and immediate future, machines will become unacceptable to the majority of Americans. I predict that in a similar way to how 2000 Mules showed how orchestrated ballot trafficking was nationally and made it easier to talk about, the Selection Code documentary[35] will open the door a deeper understanding of how the machines [s]elect candidates at the local, state, and national level.

Then, hand counting paper will be even more heavily demanded. Once trust is restored in hand counting paper ballots that are 100% auditable, maybe only then should alternatives to hand counting paper may be looked into. But let's do this patiently and persistently, one step at a time.

Read this book and share it with anyone who doesn't yet understand how machines and malicious code determine the outcome of

---

[35] https://selectioncode.com

elections in our state and country. Keep in mind this is only an introduction to the topic, as I too work daily to learn more of the details. (This book is written using a service called Leanpub, which allows the book to be reguarly updated—check back here for the latest version[36].)

Every Minnesotan deserves to know the truth. Without this information, how can the public react? And how can we hold elected officials accountable? Once the information is available, we can react. And we can hold elected officials accountable and return to a state of government of, by, and for the people.

Once the light is shone, deception and lies will no longer hold any power over us. In the domain of elections, it's not who votes or who counts the vote, it very well may be who codes the vote that matters most.

May we all be given the wisdom, strength, and discernment to carry the burden of truth. May we all with great patience endure these trials. And may we all with active persistence run the race put before us.

---

[36] https://leanpub.com/sim2020

Chapter One - Preparation

"The highest priority as a bad guy would be to subvert our election system. The reason is: you can take over a country without firing a shot. If you can decide who the leaders are, if you can put judges, if you can answer constitutional questions any way you want, over a period of time—you're not going to do it in one election, it's going to take a bunch of elections—but you can take over a country. And that would be my top priority (as a bad guy). Nuclear weapons would be a close second, but the top one would be elections."

—Jeffrey Lenberg, nation-state vulnerability expert in the May 9, 2022 Otero County, New Mexico Emergency meeting[37] who previously demonstrated vote swapping[38] in Antrim County, Michigan

---

[37] https://www.youtube.com/watch?v=Fg6Gf6QjqGM&t=939s
[38] https://rumble.com/vgi89t-hacking-democracy-antrim-county-mi-edition.html

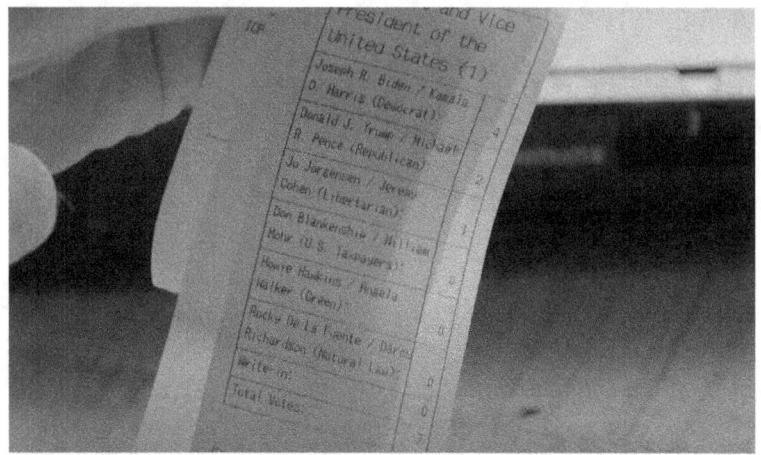

Vote Swap Demonstration in Antrim County, Michigan

As noted in the introduction, 2020 was filled with what could be called distractions but in reality were outright attacks on the American people. While those occurred, the preparation phase was shaping the battlefield. Published in 1999, a translated version of the original People's Liberation Army documents, *Un-Restricted Warfare*[39], by Col. Qiao Liang and Col. Wang Xiangsui provides context for how the George Floyd incident might relate to or be part of the same attack upon our country. In particular, chapter 7: Ten Thousand Methods Combined as One: Combinations That Transcend Boundaries, the authors argue for the necessity to exceed the previous limitations of warfare, perhaps in Machiavellian fashion going beyond acceptable methods laid down in *The United States Department of Defense Law of War Manual*[40], a guide to international humanitarian law. Qiao and Wang go on to discuss

---

[39]https://www.amazon.com/Unrestricted-Warfare-Chinas-Destroy-America/dp/1626543054

[40]https://projectapario.com/Browse?document=DQTBLMQK9&filename=DoD%20Law%20of%20War%20Manual%20-%20June%202015%20Updated%20Dec%202016.pdf

supra-national combinations, that is efforts that include national, international, and non-state organizations. The fog of war[41] makes seeing how all these elements work together difficult.

Preparation to subvert elections occurs on multiple levels, local, state, national, as well as international, not limited to the domains of law, electronic systems, and psychological operations. The unraveling of this national election theft is likely to take some time; it's implications may be difficult for some of us to comprehend, but try we must. What other option do we have?

Subversion can occur legally or illegally, constitutionally or unconstitutionally, ethically or unethically, by individuals or by coordinated groups. In the pages that follow, bear in mind that the mere fact that something is legal does not make it right. In the elections domain, a statute could be well intentioned but in practice weaken the fairness or transparency of an election. To give just one obvious example: just because ballot dropboxes found their way into state statute in a bi-partisan manner does not make drop boxes a friend of fair elections. Statutes that leave gray area present further difficulties.

In studying Minnesota election laws, one can follow the history of a particular statute over time. Did the changes to a particular statute make elections more fair or less fair? Did attempts to provide access to one vulnerable voting group such as ADA voters lead to the potential for fraud? Did judge-ordered changes amount to encasing fraud within the process itself—for instance, by what metric are signatures verified? Did the waiving of witness and signature requirements for absentee ballots make it more convenient for voters? Probably. But it also opened the door to ballot trafficking rings discovered by Gregg Phillips and Catherine Engelbrecht, highlighted in the documentary 2000 Mules.

Electronic systems must be tested, certified, and programmed prior to elections in order for them to function properly and as designed.

---

[41]https://projectapario.com/Browse?page=NKR1KBMNN&from_search_query=stumble_into

The Election Assistance Commission certified less than 6% of Minnesota counties[42] and certified none of its internet connected e-pollbooks. The DS200, a scanner and tabulator from ES&S, was used in 65 Minnesota counties, and could easily have contained 4G wireless modems, as were found in the same model of tabulator in the Antrim County, Michigan investigation[43] in late 2020 after it was discovered that thousands of votes had been flipped.

Electronic voting equipment and election management software from Dominion and Hart also had known vulnerabilities as shown at conventions like DEFCON 27 in 2019. Minnesota participates in the Electronic Registration Information Center[44](ERIC), having joined in 2014[45], which shares voter registration and other data between states, ostensibly to maintain clean voter rolls but a service which could be used to artificially inflate them. Were there any anamolies in the statewide voter registration system (SVRS) prior to or after the 2020 election in Minnesota?

In the psychological realm, in mid-2020 George Floyd dominated news cycles. Covid-19 was also a daily discussion topic on and offline. This provided distraction, air cover, and justification for procedural changes which flew in the face of existing Minnesota law.

To be covered in a later chapter, Minnesota in 2022: In the runup to 2022 elections, there have also been reports of tampering with the precinct delegate process and possible influence operations to position establishment candidates for the MNGOP endorsement and attempt to seed doubt beneath strong grassroots candidates who want to serve the interests of the people, not clandestine masters.

---

[42] https://erikvanmechelen.substack.com/p/only-6-out-of-87-counties-in-minnesota
[43] https://www.depernolaw.com/uploads/2/7/0/2/27029178/ex_5-10.pdf
[44] https://ericstates.org/
[45] https://www.minnpost.com/political-agenda/2014/09/minnesota-joins-multistate-voter-registration-group/

Minnesota Statutes and Election Law

Let's start with just a sample of Minnesota election laws and orders which affected the rules and procedures in the November 2020 general election:

1. Election day registration allowed by Minnesota Statute 201.061 Subd.3[46] (legal since 1974, when Minnesota became the second state to allow it)
2. Voter ID not required by law
3. Dropboxes for absentee and mail-in ballots allowed by Minnesota Statute 203B.082[47] (58% of 2020 votes were reportedly absentee/mail-in ballots in Minnesota, over 1.9 million votes and more than 1.2 million *more* than the prior election)
4. LaRose v. Simon - 1) Removed witness requirements for mail voters in Primary - 2) Extended the deadline to accept mail ballots (2 days) - STIPULATION AND PARTIAL CONSENT DECREE - Read LaRose Order 62 CV 20 3149 Order on July 31 Motions[48]
5. NAACP v. Simon - 1) Removed Witness Requirements for mail voters in General, 2) Extended the deadline to accept mail ballots (7 days), 3) MN Supreme Court Scheduled for September 3, 2020 - STIPULATION AND PARTIAL CONSENT DECREE - Read NAACP Order 62 CV 20 3625 Order on July 31 Motions[49]
6. This judicial complaint[50] argues Judge Sarah Grewing's decision *not* to recuse herself from above cases

---

[46] https://www.revisor.mn.gov/statutes/cite/201.061
[47] https://www.revisor.mn.gov/statutes/cite/203B.082
[48] https://www.documentcloud.org/documents/7012992-LaRose-Order-62-CV-20-3149-Order-on-July-31.html
[49] https://www.documentcloud.org/documents/7012991-NAACP-Order-62-CV-20-3625-Order-on-July-31-Motions.html
[50] https://img1.wsimg.com/blobby/go/47803963-5178-4387-9865-0ea08f5332bd/downloads/22%2003%2017%20grewing%20complaint%20with%20exhibits.pdf?ver=1648648812808

7. Minnesota Statute 206.57 Subd.6 Required Certification[51] reads in part: "…a voting system must be certified…in conformity with voluntary voting system guidelines issued by the Election Assistance Commission…" Is it true that if not in compliance with VVSG 2.0[52], voting systems are therefore not in keeping with 206.57 Subd.6 Required Certification? The EAC has not certified any independent testing laboratories to perform the "VVSG 2.0" certification. (See also the EAC's Voting System Testing and Certification Program Manual Version 3.0[53]).

> Subd. 6. **Required certification.** In addition to the requirements in subdivision 1, a voting system must be certified by an independent testing authority accredited by the Election Assistance Commission or appropriate federal agency responsible for testing and certification of compliance with the federal voting systems guidelines at the time of submission of the application required by subdivision 1 to be in conformity with voluntary voting system guidelines issued by the Election Assistance Commission or other previously referenced agency. The application must be accompanied by the certification report of the voting systems test laboratory. A certification under this section from an independent testing authority accredited by the Election Assistance Commission or other previously referenced agency meets the requirement of Minnesota Rules, part 8220.0350, item L. A vendor must provide a copy of the source code for the voting system to the secretary of state. A chair of a major political party or the secretary of state may select, in consultation with the vendor, an independent third-party evaluator to examine the source code to ensure that it functions as represented by the vendor and that the code is free from defects. A major political party that elects to have the source code examined must pay for the examination. Except as provided by this subdivision, a source code that is trade secret information must be treated as nonpublic information, according to section 13.37. A third-party evaluator must not disclose the source code to anyone else.

Are Minnesota's electronic voting systems out of compliance and therefore violating election code?

Discussion

No. 3 and No. 4 were put into motion after the MN Legislature, in April 2020, rejected Secretary of State Steve Simon's request for irrevocable power to alter election law during a pandemic.

No. 7 is included because this provides just one legal basis upon which to stand for county commissioners who choose to refuse to certify local elections in the primaries or midterm elections. It is one thing for the secretary of state to foist electronic voting equipment upon the counties. It is another thing for the county

---

[51] https://www.revisor.mn.gov/statutes/cite/206.57
[52] https://www.eac.gov/sites/default/files/TestingCertification/Voluntary_Voting_System_Guidelines_Version_2_0.pdf
[53] https://www.eac.gov/sites/default/files/TestingCertification/Testing_and_Certification_Program_Manual_Version_3_0.pdf

commissioners to certify an election just run on equipment that may violate election statutes like Minnesota Statute 206.57 Subd.6 Required Certification[54]. If county commissioners are taken to court for withholding their certification, they may ask for the machines to be opened or to examine the source code. In that event, it will be interesting to see if either request is granted.

Modern Electronic Election Systems

On January 6, 2017 the Department of Homeland Security designated elections as critical infrastructure[55], alongside food, water, and electricity.

About three months before the election, on July 28, 2020, the Cybersecurity and Infrastructure Security Agency (CISA) identified the following components as lacking security in its Critical Infrastructure Security Resilience Note[56]:

- voter registration systems
- epollbooks
- ballot preparation
- voting machines
- tabulation systems
- official websites
- storage facilities

Besides storage facilities, each of these components has undergone digitization in recent years.

Not long after the election, on November 12, 2020, CISA Assistant Director Bob Kolaksy, along with other members of the Election

---

[54] https://www.revisor.mn.gov/statutes/cite/206.57
[55] https://www.dhs.gov/news/2017/01/06/statement-secretary-johnson-designation-election-infrastructure-critical
[56] https://www.cisa.gov/sites/default/files/publications/cisa-mail-in-voting-infrastructure-risk-assessment_508.pdf

Infrastructure Government Coordinating Council (GCC) Executive Committee, made a joint statement declaring that "The November 3rd election was the most secure in American history... There is no evidence that any voting system deleted or lost votes, changed votes, or was in any way compromised."

> **JOINT STATEMENT FROM ELECTIONS INFRASTRUCTURE GOVERNMENT COORDINATING COUNCIL & THE ELECTION INFRASTRUCTURE SECTOR COORDINATING EXECUTIVE COMMITTEES**
>
> Original release date: November 12, 2020
>
> WASHINGTON – The members of Election Infrastructure Government Coordinating Council (GCC) Executive Committee – Cybersecurity and Infrastructure Security Agency (CISA) Assistant Director Bob Kolasky, U.S. Election Assistance Commission Chair Benjamin Hovland, National Association of Secretaries of State (NASS) President Maggie Toulouse Oliver, National Association of State Election Directors (NASED) President Lori Augino, and Escambia County (Florida) Supervisor of Elections David Stafford – and the members of the Election Infrastructure Sector Coordinating Council (SCC) – Chair Brian Hancock (Unisyn Voting Solutions), Vice Chair Sam Derheimer (Hart InterCivic), Chris Wlaschin (Election Systems & Software), Ericka Haas (Electronic Registration Information Center), and Maria Bianchi (Democracy Works) - released the following statement:
>
> "The November 3rd election was the most secure in American history. Right now, across the country, election officials are reviewing and double checking the entire election process prior to finalizing the result.
>
> "When states have close elections, many will recount ballots. All of the states with close results in the 2020 presidential race have paper records of each vote, allowing the ability to go back and count each ballot if necessary. This is an added benefit for security and resilience. This process allows for the identification and correction of any mistakes or errors. There is no evidence that any voting system deleted or lost votes, changed votes, or was in any way compromised.
>
> "Other security measures like pre-election testing, state certification of voting equipment, and the U.S. Election Assistance Commission's (EAC) certification of voting equipment help to build additional confidence in the voting systems used in 2020.
>
> "While we know there are many unfounded claims and opportunities for misinformation about the process of our elections, we can assure you we have the utmost confidence in the security and integrity of our elections, and you should too. When you have questions, turn to elections officials as trusted voices as they administer elections."

The most secure election, according to who?

Rick Weible, in a workshop at the Big Lake City Hall on Wednesday May 25, 2022, pointed out that this statement could not have included a review of Minnesota, since Minnesota's Canvassing Board would not certify the election until November 24, 2020 and Minnesota's election would not be certified until early December.

Further, would it be unreasonable to ask Bob Kolasky how CISA's analysis which produced the Critical Infrastructure Security and Resilience Note had changed between late July and mid November?

About a year and a half later, on June 3, 2022, CISA issued an advisory[57], "Vulnerabilities Affecting Dominion Voting Systems ImageCast X", which focuses on Dominion (but ES&S and Hart also have glaring vulnerabilities) and may have been released to get ahead of a potential leaking of the Halderman report. The advisory detailed weaknesses including hidden functionality[58] and improper

---
[57] https://www.cisa.gov/uscert/ics/advisories/icsa-22-154-01
[58] https://cwe.mitre.org/data/definitions/912.html

protection of alternate path[59]. Now, the Halderman report focuses on the internet connectivity of election equipment. But, I tend to agree with Draza Smith that we shouldn't over-focus on that given what she wrote on Telegram in March, 2022: "The thing we need to get everyone to understand is that it is the software the vendors have baked into the machines that is cheating the American people."

It's not that internet connectivity *isn't* a problem—it's a big problem because for one thing, it allows centralized real-time communication between devices. But internet-connected, networked, or remote-accessible devices aren't the only vulnerability. Even a machine *without* internet connectivity can be a huge problem for fairness and transparency based on its programming or chosen configurations.

Now, let's take the CISA-identified components one at a time.

The Statewide Voter Registration System (SVRS)

The registration files known as voter rolls or rosters are critical because they store the data which helps determine who in the state is eligible to vote. An extract of these files is pulled into the epollbooks to allow a voter to receive a ballot if voting in person on election day.

Inflated rolls facilitate ballot mules and support machine manipulation. It seems plausible that non-profits like the Electronic Registration Information Center[60] (ERIC) could provide support to states using inflated rolls through "reports that show voters who have moved within their state, voters who have moved out of state, voters who have died, duplicate registrations in the same state,

[59]https://cwe.mitre.org/data/definitions/424.html
[60]https://ericstates.org/

and individuals who are potentially eligible to vote but are not yet registered."

For instance, if member states like Minnesota do not remove voters who have moved out of state or have died, then the result is an inflated voter roll. Even if the dead or out of state voter votes, that vote technically counts since that individual will be on the statewide voter registration system with a voter ID in the system. On the second night of the Cyber Symposium, I met someone named Russ working on several problems including the problem of voters showing up in multiple states.

But how would you verify for yourself that voter rolls are inflated, providing an ample supply of ready-to-launch voters, a credit or slush fund to be used during the attack phase?

Voter rolls and histories are public information that you can request from the Minnesota Secretary of State's website[61] for $46. Note that your request is made at a particular moment in time. However, if you request a list before and after an election, as people like Rick Weible did for the November 3rd, 2020 General Election, and you are handy with database management (these are big files) then you can see how the lists changed. If you were to continue to request lists every few weeks, then you could see how the lists change over time, sometimes dramatically. (Going forward, it should not require experts in database management to hold our government accountable.)

---

[61] https://www.sos.state.mn.us/election-administration-campaigns/data-maps/registered-voter-list-requests/

Statewide Absentee Summary Data

Absentee Ballot Counts	2020 State General	2020 State Primary	2020 Presidential Primary	2018 State General	2018 State Primary	2016 State General	2016 State Primary
Transmitted	2,193,411	867,123	249,701	730,875	226,263	742,021	108,658
Returned	1,929,945	555,998	155,255	652,053	149,274	689,228	44,504
Accepted	1,909,701	543,665	145,824	638,581	143,975	676,722	42,079
Rejected	20,240	12,229	9,388	13,468	5,200	12,461	2,390

A dramatic increase in absentee ballots over time—58% of total votes in 2020, up from 25% in 2018

Historical Highs in Minnesota Absentee Votes

It was these voter rolls and histories that allowed Rick Weible to discover that more than 700,000 reported absentee votes reported by the secretary of state's website[62] were not yet connected to a voter in the SVRS on November 29, 2020, only 25 days after the election and a mere 5 days after the Minnesota State Canvassing Board certified the results[63] of the 2020 General Election.

When comparing voter rolls with census population data, one can chart turnout of the voting age population. In the following chart, we see that Minnesota ranks 1st in voting age population turnout, an indicator of fraud.

---

[62] https://www.sos.state.mn.us/election-administration-campaigns/data-maps/absentee-data/

[63] https://www.sos.state.mn.us/about-the-office/news-room/state-canvassing-board-certifies-results-of-2020-general-election/

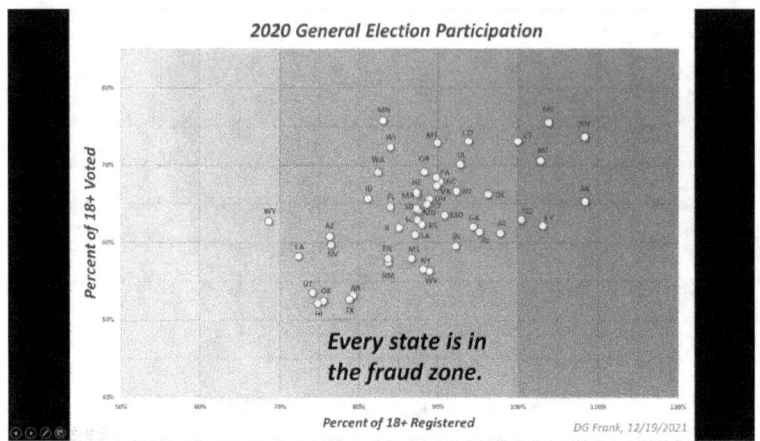

Minnesota Ranks First in Percent of 18+ Voted

The USEIP Canvassing Report[64] from March 11, 2022 visited 4,601 of 9,472 residences in Douglas, El Paso, Pueblo, and Weld Counties, Colorado. They found that about 8% of voters (123,852 of 1.1M) were affected by unexplained irregularities in Colorado's voter rolls and voting records.

This rate of irregularities was similar to a 30-county canvassing effort led by Robin Sylvester in Minnesota, which so far has canvassed about 2,000 homes and found just under 300 suspicious records.

In neighboring Wisconsin, Jeffrey O'Donnell's analysis of data from August 2021 voter rolls[65] showed over 7 million separate voter records in a state with less than 6 million people.

Rick Weible has acquired voter rolls and histories from multiple states. When examined collectively, the inflation either inspired by or influenced directly by organizations like the Electronic Registration Information Center (ERIC) is plain to see. We have since learned that there is a connection between Soros-funded Catalist

---

[64]https://useipdotus.files.wordpress.com/2022/03/useip-colorado-canvassing-report.pdf
[65]https://magaraccoon.com/docs/wisconsin1.pdf

and ERIC[66] which helps to decrease the number of people on ERIC's 'Eligible but Unregistered' EBU list. According to the EAVS report compiled by the EAC, there were 103,701,513 registration applications[67] between the close of registration in 2018 and the close of registration in 2020, a 4x increase for the equivalent timeframe for the 2016 general election. The result of helping people become registered leads to head-scratching outomces like this in California.

State	County 2000	Total Registrations	CVAP	Total Reg. as Pct. of CVAP
CALIFORNIA	ALPINE COUNTY	982	815	120.5%
CALIFORNIA	LOS ANGELES COUNTY	7,122,542	6,319,285	112.7%
CALIFORNIA	SAN MATEO COUNTY	554,665	501,484	110.6%
CALIFORNIA	SOLANO COUNTY	338,764	309,099	109.6%
CALIFORNIA	SANTA CRUZ COUNTY	210,731	192,861	109.3%
CALIFORNIA	SAN DIEGO COUNTY	2,437,272	2,265,800	107.6%
CALIFORNIA	SISKIYOU COUNTY	35,949	33,760	106.5%
CALIFORNIA	SANTA CLARA COUNTY	1,243,464	1,175,132	105.8%
CALIFORNIA	VENTURA COUNTY	594,523	563,242	105.6%
CALIFORNIA	STANISLAUS COUNTY	356,744	329,433	105.1%
CALIFORNIA	NEVADA COUNTY	84,137	80,115	105.0%
CALIFORNIA	IMPERIAL COUNTY	108,397	103,885	104.3%
CALIFORNIA	YUBA COUNTY	53,193	51,018	104.3%
CALIFORNIA	YOLO COUNTY	149,469	145,380	102.5%
CALIFORNIA	EL DORADO COUNTY	147,198	143,861	102.3%
CALIFORNIA	PLACER COUNTY	290,409	285,075	101.9%
CALIFORNIA	SAN BENITO COUNTY	38,975	38,329	101.7%
CALIFORNIA	MARIN COUNTY	188,059	185,230	101.5%
CALIFORNIA	SACRAMENTO	1,049,495	1,041,824	100.7%
CALIFORNIA	SHASTA COUNTY	136,598	136,211	100.3%
CALIFORNIA	ALAMEDA COUNTY	1,084,410	1,083,648	100.1%
CALIFORNIA	ORANGE COUNTY	2,061,672	2,060,449	100.1%
CALIFORNIA	MODOC COUNTY	6,751	6,765	99.8%
CALIFORNIA	CALAVERAS COUNTY	36,532	36,843	99.2%
CALIFORNIA	SIERRA COUNTY	2,472	2,506	98.6%
CALIFORNIA	MONTEREY COUNTY	226,045	231,872	97.5%
CALIFORNIA	FRESNO COUNTY	573,873	588,878	97.5%
CALIFORNIA	CONTRA COSTA COUNTY	735,818	761,019	96.7%
CALIFORNIA	LAKE COUNTY	46,177	47,962	96.3%
CALIFORNIA	HUMBOLDT COUNTY	102,265	106,325	96.2%
CALIFORNIA	MERCED COUNTY	144,364	150,155	96.1%
CALIFORNIA	SANTA BARBARA COUNTY	268,594	281,934	95.3%
CALIFORNIA	SUTTER COUNTY	58,285	61,221	95.2%
CALIFORNIA	SAN BERNARDINO COUNTY	1,294,038	1,364,253	94.9%
CALIFORNIA	SAN FRANCISCO COUNTY	616,670	652,449	94.5%
CALIFORNIA	RIVERSIDE COUNTY	1,463,308	1,555,774	94.1%
CALIFORNIA	SAN LUIS OBISPO COUNTY	204,736	218,760	93.6%
CALIFORNIA	NAPA COUNTY	88,300	95,556	92.4%
CALIFORNIA	AMADOR COUNTY	29,251	31,698	92.3%
CALIFORNIA	MARIPOSA COUNTY	12,946	14,101	91.8%
CALIFORNIA	KERN COUNTY	477,886	521,859	91.6%
CALIFORNIA	MENDOCINO COUNTY	56,493	62,192	90.8%
CALIFORNIA	SAN JOAQUIN	416,153	458,995	90.7%
CALIFORNIA	PLUMAS COUNTY	13,704	15,228	90.0%
CALIFORNIA	TULARE COUNTY	230,719	256,924	89.8%
CALIFORNIA	MONO COUNTY	8,788	9,866	89.1%
CALIFORNIA	INYO COUNTY	12,037	13,605	88.5%
CALIFORNIA	TEHAMA COUNTY	40,241	45,884	87.7%
CALIFORNIA	MADERA COUNTY	80,595	91,909	87.7%
CALIFORNIA	TRINITY COUNTY	8,948	10,227	87.5%
CALIFORNIA	GLENN COUNTY	15,025	17,298	86.9%
CALIFORNIA	DEL NORTE COUNTY	17,789	20,579	86.4%
CALIFORNIA	TUOLUMNE COUNTY	37,998	44,215	85.9%
CALIFORNIA	BUTTE COUNTY	148,013	173,139	85.5%
CALIFORNIA	SONOMA COUNTY	300,586	357,328	84.1%
CALIFORNIA	COLUSA COUNTY	10,070	12,366	81.4%
CALIFORNIA	KINGS COUNTY	69,084	93,191	74.1%
CALIFORNIA	LASSEN COUNTY	15,414	25,071	61.5%
Total		26,157,616	25,494,383	102.6%

102.6% of California Citizens of Voting Age are Registered to Vote

Minnesota is not much better, with for instance Carver County having *more* registered voters than citizens of voting age population, which should not happen.

---

[66]https://andmagazine.substack.com/p/whats-the-connection-between-eric
[67]https://www.eac.gov/sites/default/files/document_library/files/2020_EAVS_Report_Final_508c.pdf

91.7% of Minnesotan Citizens of Voting Age are Registered to Vote

Epollbooks

Epollbooks are generally connected to the internet so that they can both receive a precinct-level extract of the statewide voter registration system or are at minimum a digital file if not connected or networked. The internet connection also provides for real-time updating which conceivably would have allowed the Minnesota Attorney General to make a certain tweet at 3:57pm[68] on election day, which may have been a signal to the ballot mules.

---

[68]https://twitter.com/keithellison/status/1323746158557253632

Keith Ellison ✓
@keithellison

If you've voted, great! Can you please call a friend? Spend a little time getting friends, fams, and folks out to the polls. We don't have all of the votes we need quite yet. So, help a friend (even a brand new friend) vote. Right now would be awesome.

3:57 PM · Nov 3, 2020 · Twitter for iPhone

188 Retweets   **876** Quote Tweets   **953** Likes

This Tweet is from a suspended account. Learn more

Shawn Olson 🔥 @OOOlson · Nov 3, 2020
This tweet won't age well

♡ 22   ⟲ 2   ♡ 32

This tweet hasn't aged well

As recently as the New Jersey primaries in early June 2022, evidence of the Nighthawk providing internet connectivity to 8 Tenex epollbooks was documented at one polling place. For the first three hours, no one noticed. Then, the county board of elections office called one of the senior poll workers on her cell phone to remind her to set up the Nighthawk because prior to that the board officials were unable to monitor the processing of voters.

Real Time Monitoring of Processing of Voters

In 2016, when Rick Weible was the mayor of St. Bonifacius, he hacked into the proposed epollbook within minutes. Then he declined to sign a contract to use them in St. Bonifacius. His was the only city in Hennepin County *not* to use epollbooks (they used paper pollbooks) in the following election.

As shown on the Verified Voting website[69], the majority if not all of Minnesota's counties use the KNOWiNK Poll Pads, which are essentially converted iPads for epollbook use. These electronic poll pads are not certified by the Election Assistance Commission (EAC). Rick Weible has spoken about cloud issues that were documented in Sherburne County[70] on election day, 2020.

Ballot Preparation

Ballot preparation is a complicated process. But Patrick Colbeck does us a favor of simplifying the complex in his book, *The 2020 Coup*:

"Ballots are another key election infrastructure component with security vulnerabilities. Modern ballots are much more sophisticated than a piece of paper with checkboxes next to names. Today's ballots are sophisticated paper and/or digital documents. In fact, in some cases, ballots are replaced by Direct-Recording Electronic (DRE) voting machines.

---

[69]https://verifiedvoting.org/verifier/#mode/navigate/map/ppEquip/mapType/normal/year/2022/state/27

[70]https://rumble.com/v19obfd-cloud-issues-with-electronic-poll-pads-in-sherburne-county.html

Sample Ballot Image with watermark applied:

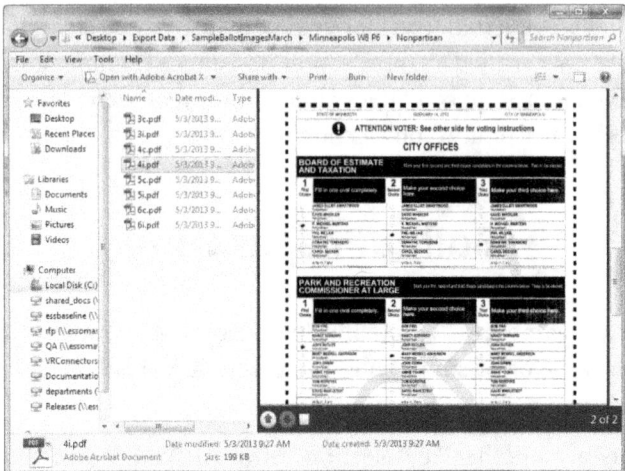

Sample ballot image

"Ballot preparation is a complicated process of overlaying political geographies with the contests and candidates specific to each district and then translating those layouts into unique combinations of ballot data. Ballot preparation data takes multiple forms such as ballot images (both paper and electronic), the data files necessary to build ballot images, audio files for special use ballots, and specific files for export to external systems such as websites for Uniformed and Overseas Citizens Absentee Voting Act (UOCAVA)-focused digital systems. Ballot preparation also generates the data necessary for tabulating votes within a voting machine and aggregating tabulated votes within a jurisdiction or state. This process is usually completed in an election documents and records management system (EDRMS), which is special software designed to manage documents and records throughout the document lifecycle, from creation to destruction. Access to the information in such systems would enable anyone attempting to subert the integrity of an election with the information necessary to create ballots independently of election officials. Of course, ballots are also where voters record their votes. Vote tallies are generated from the information on ballots therefore their integrity is very important to protect."

After watching 2000 Mules Erin Clements asked where the NGOs that printed the ballots for the mules may have gotten the ballot formatting and ballot styles to correctly print ballots. I imagine True the Vote's Catherine Engelbrecht and Gregg Phillips' team were asking the same questions, leading to their follow-on work from the Wisconsin hearing in March 2022 to the Maricopa County senate hearing in early June to the work on the ground in Yuma County.

While Minnesota uses paper ballots in all 87 counties, we are *not* hand-counting them. Because there is no hand tally, we are putting our trust completely in the voting machines and tabulation systems to properly scan, tally, and record the votes on each paper ballot and the aggregation of those totals. The voting machines, also called tabulators, scan and tally the votes. Simply put—but the process is anything *but* simple—the tallies from the tabulators are then aggregated in tabulation software known as an election management system. Results from this election management system are then supposed to be passed through reporting providers like Edison Research and eventually through the media to your living room. However, Jeffrey O'Donnell and Draza Smith have speculated that this election night reporting could well be theater and not directly connected to actual results recorded in tabulators.

Voting Machines

The most common voting machines is otherwise known as a tabulator. These optical scanners take in paper ballots and then are essentially interpreting pixels on a bitmap and translating that into vote tallies.

Vendors largely keep to themselves their standards for interpreting ovals. In certain situations, the tabulators are programmed to send ballots to adjudication, where election judges are responsible (not the voter) for deciding the intent of the voter. This includes situations like blank ballots, overvotes, ambiguous marks, and ballot misreads.

It's conceivable that these tabulators make mistakes that humans would not make. Erin Clements demonstrated evidence of this[71] from the Otero County audit in the Otero County Special Meeting on June 9, 2022. She concluded, "The tabulators are not smarter than people."

In that same audit, there was a software mismatch between the tabulators and the election management system (a violation of the election code in New Mexico law), and yet the mismatch did not prevent the tabulation systems from processing vote tallies.

Here is a table of electronic voting equipment used in Minnesota's 2020 general election, provided by Dan Sundin, part of the decentralized Telegram group mentioned in the introduction, who despite not living in Minnesota did me a favor and pulled this information from each of the county websites (in addition to precinct-level results for all counties).

County Name	Absentee and Mail Ballot Tabulation Equipment	Assistive Voting Equipment
Aitkin	ImageCast Central	ImageCast Evolution
Anoka	Digital Scan 200, Digital Scan 450, Digital Scan 850	AutoMARK
Becker	Model 100	AutoMARK
Beltrami	Digital Scan 200, Digital Scan 450	AutoMARK

---

[71] https://www.youtube.com/watch?v=Z_2SNcUSdlI

County Name	Absentee and Mail Ballot Tabulation Equipment	Assistive Voting Equipment
Benton	Digital Scan 450	AutoMARK
Big Stone	Verity Scan	Verity Touch Writer
Blue Earth	Digital Scan 200, Digital Scan 450	OmniBallot
Brown	Digital Scan 450	AutoMARK
Carlton	Digital Scan 200	AutoMARK
Carver	Digital Scan 200, Digital Scan 450	AutoMARK
Cass	Digital Scan 200, Digital Scan 450	OmniBallot
Chippewa	Digital Scan 200	AutoMARK
Chisago	Verity Central, Verity Scan	Verity Touch Writer
Clay	Digital Scan 200, Digital Scan 450	AutoMARK
Clearwater	Digital Scan 200	AutoMARK
Cook	Digital Scan 200	AutoMARK
Cottonwood	Digital Scan 200	AutoMARK
Crow Wing	ImageCast Central	ImageCast Evolution
Dakota	ImageCast Central	ImageCast Evolution
Dodge	Digital Scan 200	AutoMARK
Douglas	Digital Scan 200, Digital Scan 450	OmniBallot
Faribault	Digital Scan 200	AutoMARK
Fillmore	Digital Scan 200	AutoMARK
Freeborn	Digital Scan 200, Digital Scan 450	AutoMARK
Goodhue	Digital Scan 450	AutoMARK
Grant	Digital Scan 200	AutoMARK
Hennepin	Digital Scan 200, Digital Scan 850	AutoMARK
Houston	Digital Scan 200	AutoMARK
Hubbard	Digital Scan 450	OmniBallot

County Name	Absentee and Mail Ballot Tabulation Equipment	Assistive Voting Equipment
Isanti	Digital Scan 200	OmniBallot
Itasca	Digital Scan 200	OmniBallot
Jackson	Digital Scan 200	OmniBallot
Kanabec	Digital Scan 200	AutoMARK
Kandiyohi	Digital Scan 200	AutoMARK
Kittson	Digital Scan 450	AutoMARK
Koochiching	Digital Scan 200	AutoMARK
Lac Qui Parle	Digital Scan 450	OmniBallot
Lake	Digital Scan 200	AutoMARK
Lake Of The Woods	Digital Scan 200	OmniBallot
Le Sueur	Digital Scan 200	AutoMARK
Lincoln	Digital Scan 200	AutoMARK
Lyon	Digital Scan 200	AutoMARK
Mcleod	Digital Scan 200, Digital Scan 450	AutoMARK
Mahnomen	ImageCast Evolution	ImageCast Evolution
Marshall	Digital Scan 850	AutoMARK
Martin	Digital Scan 200, Digital Scan 450	AutoMARK
Meeker	Digital Scan 200	OmniBallot
Mille Lacs	Digital Scan 200	AutoMARK
Morrison	Digital Scan 200, Digital Scan 450	AutoMARK
Mower	Digital Scan 200	AutoMARK
Murray	Digital Scan 200	AutoMARK
Nicollet	Digital Scan 200	AutoMARK
Nobles	Digital Scan 200	AutoMARK
Norman	Digital Scan 200	AutoMARK
Olmsted	Digital Scan 850	AutoMARK
Otter Tail	Digital Scan 200	AutoMARK
Pennington	Digital Scan 200	AutoMARK
Pine	Digital Scan 200, Model 100	AutoMARK

County Name	Absentee and Mail Ballot Tabulation Equipment	Assistive Voting Equipment
Pipestone	Digital Scan 200	OmniBallot
Polk	Digital Scan 450	OmniBallot, AutoMARK
Pope	Digital Scan 200	AutoMARK
Ramsey	Digital Scan 850, Verity Central, Verity Scan	Verity Touch Writer, AutoMARK
Red Lake	Digital Scan 200	AutoMARK
Redwood	Digital Scan 200	AutoMARK
Renville	Digital Scan 200	AutoMARK
Rice	Digital Scan 200, Digital Scan 450	AutoMARK
Rock	Digital Scan 200	OmniBallot
Roseau	Digital Scan 200	OmniBallot
St. Louis	Digital Scan 200, Digital Scan 850, Model 100	AutoMARK
Scott	ImageCast Central, ImageCast Evolution	ImageCast Evolution
Sherburne	ImageCast Central	ImageCast Evolution
Sibley	Digital Scan 200	AutoMARK
Stearns	Digital Scan 450, Digital Scan 850	AutoMARK
Steele	Digital Scan 200	AutoMARK
Stevens	Digital Scan 200	AutoMARK
Swift	Digital Scan 200	OmniBallot
Todd	Digital Scan 200	OmniBallot
Traverse	Digital Scan 200	AutoMARK
Wabasha	Digital Scan 200	AutoMARK
Wadena	Digital Scan 200	AutoMARK
Waseca	Digital Scan 200	OmniBallot, AutoMARK

County Name	Absentee and Mail Ballot Tabulation Equipment	Assistive Voting Equipment
Washington	Digital Scan 850, Verity Central	Verity Touch Writer, AutoMARK
Watonwan	Digital Scan 200	AutoMARK
Wilkin	Digital Scan 200	OmniBallot
Winona	Digital Scan 200	AutoMARK
Wright	Digital Scan 200, Digital Scan 450	AutoMARK
Yellow Medicine	Digital Scan 200	AutoMARK

Another way to view which equipment was in use in 2020 or will be in use for 2022 is on the Verified Voting website[72].

Remember, there are known and potential vulnerabilities in all voting machines, but let's zoom in for a moment on the most-used equipment in Minnesota.

ES&S DS200s were used in 65 of Minnesota's 87 counties in 2020.

In April 2021, the DS200 used in Antrim, County Michigan was found to have a 4G wireless modem installed[73] within the enclosure of the machine.

---

[72] https://verifiedvoting.org/verifier/#mode/navigate/map/ppEquip/mapType/normal/year/2022/state/27

[73] https://letsfixstufforg-my.sharepoint.com/personal/patrick_letsfixstuff_org/_layouts/15/onedrive.aspx?id=%2Fpersonal%2Fpatrick%5Fletsfixstuff%5Forg%2FDocuments%2FFiles%2F2020%20Election%2FLegal%2FExhibit%206%20Jim%20Penrose%20Report%2Epdf&parent=%2Fpersonal%2Fpatrick%5Fletsfixstuff%5Forg%2FDocuments%2FFiles%2F2020%20Election%2FLegal&ga=1

Telit LE910-SV1 found within ES&S enclosure

Furthermore, the exhibit describes[74] how the card was "utilizing a commercial Verizon SIM card with an APN configuration specific to the ES&S DS200 provisioning. Testing revealed that the same SIM card could be utilized in a separate wireless hotspot device and the device could then join the same APN as the ES&S voting machines. An unauthorized user could gain access to this APN by an extra SIM card pre-provisioned for this APN, or by removing a SIM from an operational device and using it in another device."

To repeat: This wireless modem was found on an enclosed part of the machine. Therefore if these same or similar wireless modems were also installed on the DS200s throughout Minnesota, it would be invisible to election judges, poll challengers, and even election officials regardless of whether the machiens were certified. Under Minnesota law, it is not required that every machine be certified, only the model of machine. (From 206.57 Subd.1[75], "Examination is not required of every individual machine or counting device.") Testing can be limited to certain requirements which evidently can

---

[74]https://letsfixstufforg-my.sharepoint.com/personal/patrick_letsfixstuff_org/_layouts/15/onedrive.aspx?id=%2Fpersonal%2Fpatrick%5Fletsfixstuff%5Forg%2FDocuments%2FFiles%2F2020%20Election%2FLegal%2FExhibit%206%20Jim%20Penrose%20Report%2Epdf&parent=%2Fpersonal%2Fpatrick%5Fletsfixstuff%5Forg%2FDocuments%2FFiles%2F2020%20Election%2FLegal&ga=1

[75]https://www.revisor.mn.gov/statutes/cite/206.57

miss the presence of a 4G wireles modem.

The presence of these would seem to also disqualify a voting system according to the VVSG 2.0[76] (relevant to county commissioners considering whether to certify their upcoming local elections):

> **Internal Wireless Networks**
>
> Internal wireless networks wirelessly communicate or transfer information between two or more devices. Examples include use of wireless (Bluetooth) mice and keyboards or (Wi-Fi) printers. There are also growing trends towards using wireless technology for assistive devices such as headsets or hearing aids.
>
> Wireless technology within the voting system introduces security concerns in that wireless networks can provide an entry point to the voting system for attackers. The security configurations for devices used in wireless technologies are not all equally secure, with some configured to provide more strength than others.
>
> The *VVSG 2.0* requires that a voting system be incapable of broadcasting a wireless network (see *14.2-C – Wireless communication restrictions* and *15.4-C – Documentation for disabled*
>
> Requirements for VVSG 2.0   13   February 10, 2021

Voting systems should be incapable of broadcasting a wireless network

I also include this information in the preparation phase of our discussion because this 4G wireless modem implementation would likely need to be installed *before* or *during* the election in order to be used by bad actors.

Additionally, scientist Dr. Douglas Frank has called the ES&S DS200[77] "one of the most hackable ballot scanners in the country". Because the code is not open source, it is difficult to know all the vulnerabilities that may exist. And since its "System and Method for Decoding Marks on a Paper Ballot" is proprietary, patent law means ES&S owns that intellectual property. That being said, former cyber analyst for the Air Force Jake Stauffer's vulnerability report[78] is revealing, demonstrating among other details that "file systems

---

[76] https://www.eac.gov/sites/default/files/TestingCertification/Voluntary_Voting_System_Guidelines_Version_2_0.pdf
[77] https://t.me/FollowTheData/1985
[78] https://www.scribd.com/document/513400991/ESS-RedTeam-Jake-Stauffer-Vulnerability-Security-Assessment-Report

are not encrypted [which] allowed the team to recover system configuration information, password hashes, and ES&S specific binaries."

To understand how the DS200 plays into the overall system, here's a diagram ES&S sent to Travis County, Texas in a contract proposal.

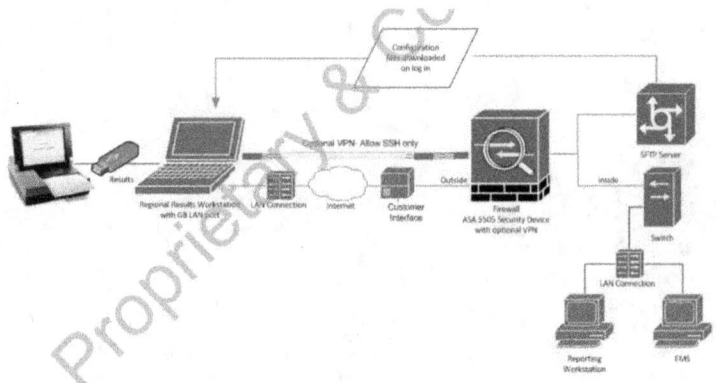

ES&S DIAGRAM THE COMPANY SUBMITTED LAST YEAR TO TRAVIS COUNTY, TEXAS, AS PART OF A CONTRACT PROPOSAL SHOWS THE REPORTING SYSTEM AND ELECTION-MANAGEMENT SYSTEM DIRECTLY CONNECTED TO THE SFTP SERVER THROUGH THE SWITCH, AND ALL OF THEM ARE CONNECTED TO THE FIREWALL.

Part of an ES&S contract proposal sent to Travis County, Texas

To make matters worse, however, there are apparently settings on the DS200 which allow the ballot images to *not* be saved (reducing the audit trail) and potentially configuration settings which turn off the Cast Vote Record (CVR) report functionality, though the details of this are still being verified. (Edit: See Chapter Four - Defense, for verification, including a screenshot from the ES&S DS200 Operator Guide.)

If true, (edit: it *is* true) this is a big problem because it turns off the machines' ability to tell on itself. Where this decision was made, it may have ultimately prevented voters from learning whether the machine-recorded vote tallies matched their paper ballot submissions. (The outputs of CVR reports will be used in the backup attack phase and defense phase chapters because of how *key* they are.)

Turning off the functionality to generate CVRs may also have explained why Minnesotans sending public data requests have been met with letters like this one from the Todd County Attorney.

CHARLES G. RASMUSSEN
Todd County Attorney

Jane M. Gustafson
John E. Lindemann
Heidi E. Schultz
Christopher D. Mathews
Assistant County Attorneys

221 1st Avenue South, Suite 400, Long Prairie, MN 56347
Phone: 320-732-6039 Fax: 320-732-4120
toddcountyattorney@co.todd.mn.us

March 24, 2022

Denise Gaida
Auditor/Treasurer
Todd County Courthouse
Long Prairie, MN 56347

RE: Eric Van Mechelen Email Requests

Dear Denise:

I have reviewed the string of e-mails concerning Mr. Erik van Mechelen's request for CVR cast vote record reports for the November 2020 election. It is my understanding that Todd County does not create this data nor does it have such data stored anywhere. Chapter 13 does not require Todd County to create any data if it does not exist. Therefore, since Todd County does not have this data, it cannot comply with the request. Thank you.

Sincerely,

Charles G. Rasmussen
Todd County Attorney

/smp

The opinion of the Todd County Attorney

Please note that although we have focused on the ES&S DS200s, there are several Minnesota counties that use Dominion Image-Cast machines and several that use Hart Verity Scan tabulators. Equipment from these vendors are also insecure from cyber threats. More importantly, vendors are not open with their source code and therefore vote-manipulating software could be baked in. That said, any commissioners opting to withhold their certifications of local elections could request a micro-audit, to be performed in under a day, of their voting machines to ensure that security and accuracy were maintained throughout the election.

Tabulation Systems

Here again I lean on Patrick Colbeck's description, this time from page 10 in *The 2020 Coup*:

"Tabulators are critical election infrastructure components with significant security vulnerabilities. At the precinct-level, tabulators are used to read a ballot, convert the ballot image to votes, and add the vote data on a given ballot to the running tally of votes stored in a digital table. Precint-level vote tallies are then aggregated by centralized vote tabulation systems at the municipal, county, and state levels. Collectively, these systems help determine and communicate the results of an election. If tabulators are compromised, they can shift votes from one candidate to another. These votes shifts can change the results of an election."

Dan Sundin's description of ES&S's ElectionWare is helpful to understand how important the tabulation system is:

"ElectionWare runs in the Server computer (which may just be a workstation depending upon the customer deliverable). ElectionWare is key, as it does all the related work in generating the Election Project Files, the optioning of the races, districts, precincts and splits of those precincts. It downloads the related information in to all of the collection points, ExpressVote BMD, DS200 Scanners at the precincts, and sets up the Central Count Site Scanners, DS450, DS850 and now DS950. It also creates all the PDF Ballot files for professional printing and for creation via the Ballot-on-Demand print feature."

The following diagram shows how five elements of the ES&S EVS tabulation system is put together, which include:

1. Election Data Management
2. Ballot Formatting and Printing
3. Voting Equipment Configuration
4. Voting and Tabulation

5. Results Consolidation and Reporting

The Complicated System Configuration of ES&S Electionware

In the 3/15/2022 Nye County, Nevada County Commissioner's meeting[79] cyber security consultant Mark Cook described his experience[80] with computers pre-internet in the CompuServe and Prodigy days, then as a consultant to protect companies from threats and seal off vulnerability, and finally with election systems.

Today, Dominion is a popular voting system which uses Microsoft SQL database, one which Mark was and is very familiar with as he used SQL databases from day 1. In the same meeting, he discussed how within the first minute of getting his hands on a Dominion system, he was able to access the backend and change votes...without leaving a trace.

In the Antrim County, Michigan investigation, where there were a confirmed 7,000 votes flipped (in the 2020 election), nation-state vulnerability expert Jeff Lenberg demonstrated vote swapping[81] that

---
[79] https://www.youtube.com/watch?t=234&v=GBKz1o_VqAE&feature=youtu.be
[80] https://www.youtube.com/watch?v=GBKz1o_VqAE&t=234s
[81] https://rumble.com/vgi89t-hacking-democracy-antrim-county-mi-edition.html

allowed the election management system and tabulator printouts to match (for the canvass). The problem? The EMS and the tabulator tapes would not match the paper ballots initially scanned through the tabulator. (This is still one of my favorite videos and mirrors a mock election experience that Draza Smith, Col. Shawn Smith, and Mark Cook created alongside Patrick Colbeck at the Cyber Symposium. Once you see how easy it is to swap votes, it cannot be unseen, and this is only one of many exploitable vulnerabilities.)

In 2021, when Tina Peters learned that a Dominion vendor was planning to visit her office to make a software update, she took action in line with her statutory duties to preserve election data as the Mesa County Clerk. She worked with consultants to save a copy of the before and after image of her Dominion Voting Systems (DVS) Election Management System (EMS) servers, which data analysts then began investigating to detect what Dominion's "Trusted Build" may have changed.

It turned out to be a lot.

The Mesa County Colorado Voting Systems Report #3: Election Database and Data Process Analysis[82] proves database manipulation happened inside the Colorado Dominion Voting Systems (DVS) Election Management System (EMS). Not once, but twice, in both the 2020 General Election and the 2021 Grand Junction Municipal Election. (The first report[83] and the second report[84] are also very useful.)

The third report has been called the "Rosetta Stone" by one of its authors because it provided the fingerprints of the nefarious activity and will be featured in the Selection Code[85] documentary.

These not so trust-worthy software updates were performed by Dominion employees across the country, possibly destroying evidence of election tampering and manipulation. It is possible that such

---

[82] https://magaraccoon.com/docs/MesaCountyReport3.pdf
[83] http://kevinlundberg.com/wp-content/uploads/2021/09/Exhibit-F.pdf
[84] https://useipdotus.files.wordpress.com/2022/03/mesa-county-forensic-report-no.-2.pdf
[85] https://selectioncode.com

an update may have occurred in the six Minnesota counties using the Domininon Voting System (DVS) Election Management System (EMS). So far, just the one before/after image of the servers exists, truly a God send.

Influence Operations

I have chosen to borrow the term *influence operations* from Patrick Colbeck since it is less frequently used when compared to *psychological operations* or *psyops*. The screens which bring us our daily inspiration and fear, information from loved ones and our 2-minute's hate (à la *1984*), are seemingly a blessing and a curse.

A blessing because it is only with the internet that information can be shared quickly enough and widely enough to outflank centralized media platforms and censorship regimes.

But a curse because influence operations are deployed on those screens which provide an unobstructed path to our brain, unless one is armored up and discerning wisely.

For me, the most significant influence operations in the preparation phase in Minnesota were George Floyd, its extended aftermath, and of course, Covid-19.

At the time I lived not far from 38th and Chicago.

A few months later, I biked there once and another time went on foot. Roads were blocked making it difficult for locals to leave area in cars. Shops were closed replaced by vendors selling t-shirts and BLM masks. Flowers were laid before the provocative murals and around the monument at the intersection.

In the days following May 25, 2022, there were protests and looting and riots. The 3rd precinct police station burned. It was a trying time to the point that I even asked one of my clients if I could take time off from a gig. One protest organized by Royce White, now a candidate for Congress in CD5[86], went to the Federal Reserve, an interesting and significant choice that got the attention of many, though I missed it at the time.

Covid-19 led to the deployment of eerily similar lockdowns and language worldwide. The monthly discussion groups I'd held ended and I resorted for a time to arguing needlessly with friends online. One day I saw Jacob Frey, Mayor of Minneapolis, jogging maskless near the fairly crowded Stone Arch Bridge—that evening he was wearing a mask announcing new recommendations and rules. Then came the experimental vaccines, only qualifying to be called as such because of dictionaries redefining the term. Perhaps suspecting I had exercised my right not to partake, a Mayo Clinic ICU doctor before a pickup soccer game asked if I had questions about Covid-19. It was great to see people like Lisa Hanson defy shutdown orders[87] and unfairly spend 60 days in jail[88] and people like Mark Bishofsky organize rallies[89] at the St. Paul Capitol. When Mayor Frey and Mayor Carter announced in a joint press conference the vaccine card requirements, I wrote this article[90] questioning their judgment. Months later, I was on the phone with the head of a hospital in Seattle who predicted that the inventors of the mRNA vaccines would get Nobel prizes. Maybe they will. But so did Barrack Hussein Obama (*before* many realized what he was up to). When I asked this head of hospital if he got his booster, he said he probably wouldn't get the next one.

The chaos played into the enemy's hands.

The subversion of our elections was well under way.

All the while, preparations continued to be made for the election

---

[86] https://roycewhite.us/

[87] https://minnesota.cbslocal.com/2021/12/10/bar-owner-who-defied-covid-orders-sentenced-to-90-days-in-jail/

[88] https://rumble.com/v17opq6-now-its-my-turn-so-it-never-happens-again-the-lisa-hanson-story.html

[89] https://theminnesotasun.com/2021/09/28/thousands-attended-medical-freedom-rally-featuring-del-bigtree/

[90] https://erikvanmechelen.substack.com/p/as-coronavirus-narrative-collapses

with little if any reporting of substance regarding the consent decrees which stripped witness and signature requirements from absentee ballots, nor the mass installment of Zuckerboxes, nor the preparations the work of True the Vote has shone light upon in the first half of 2022.

As part of the Attack Phase, to that we turn next.

Chapter Two - Attack

"It's an organized crime. It was perpetrated on Americans by advancing bad process: dirty voter rolls, ballot boxes, all sorts of mail-in ballot capabilities. And you roll all that up and it's quite evident to those of us who've spent the last 15 months of our lives developing these numbers that this was indeed an organized crime that was perpetrated on Americans."

—Gregg Phillips in the informational hearing[91](see 32:32 time stamp) before the Assembly Committee on Campaigns and Elections in Madison, Wisconsin on March 24, 2022.

By now many are familiar with suitcases of ballots being scanned by Ruby Freeman or the truckloads of ballots being delivered to the TCF Center in Detroit. But to understand the scale of the attack on the weakest part of the American election system—absentee and mail-in ballots—let's first review a few high level statistics.

In the EAC's 2020 Election Administration and Voting Survey[92] (EAVS), the following stats are given in on page 1 of Chapter 1. Overview of Election Administration and Voting in the 2020 General election:

- More than 209 million people were active registered voters for the 2020 general election, an all-time high for the EAVS.

---

[91]https://www.truethevote.org/election-integrity-testimony-in-wisconsin-on-thursday-march-24-2022/

[92]https://www.eac.gov/sites/default/files/document_library/files/2020_EAVS_Report_Final_508c.pdf

- Voter turnout for the 2020 general election reached the highest level documented in any EAVS thus far, at 67.7% of the citizen voting age population (CVAP). Turnout increased 6.7 percentage points from 2016 levels, and nearly all states reported an increase in turnout. More than 161 million voters cast ballots that were counted for the 2020 election.
- For the first time, a majority of voters cast their ballots before Election Day. Slightly more than 43% of voters participated with a mailed ballot, and 30.6% of ballots were cast through in-person voting before Election Day. Ballots cast on Election Day at a physical polling place comprised 30.5% of the turnout for the 2020 general election.
- The number of mailed ballots transmitted to voters more than doubled from 2016 to 2020, and the percentage of mailed ballots that were returned by voters, that were counted, and that were rejected held steady with 2016 levels.

It is now a proven fact that ballot harvesting and more critically ballot *trafficking* operations were in effect across the country throughout the 2020 election.

In Minnesota we perhaps caught a small glimpse of ballot harvesting through the Project Veritas reporting on Ilhan-Omar connected ballot harvesting schemes[93] in September 2020. However, the ballot harvesting being done in those videos only sheds light on traditional ballot harvesting—notable but not highlighting the scale of operations likely at work in Minnesota—in that case exploiting the elderly in apartment towers for which the in-person polling place was within walking distance if not in the same building.

What True the Vote's work showed—which in my opinion was only glimpsed in documentaries like 2000 Mules—is that a likely nationwide coordinated effort to print ballots at NGOs and have them dropped off in drop boxes (or the mail) by paid mules. This is

---

[93]https://www.projectveritas.com/news/ilhan-omar-connected-cash-for-ballots-voter-fraud-scheme-corrupts-elections/

ballot *trafficking*, what Gregg Phillips called "organized crime that was perpetrated on Americans."

True the Vote's election integrity report[94] titled "Delivery of Absentee Ballots by Intermediaries to Milwaukee County Area Drop Boxes October 20 – November 3, 2020 was published on March 18, 2022. A week later, in Madison, Wisconsin, Catherine Engelbrecht and Gregg Phillips gave testimony in an informational hearing[95] before the Assembly Committee on Campaigns and Elections.

From the True the Vote (TTV) report:

"In 2021, in response to whistleblower reports, TTV began purchasing and analyzing publicly available drop box surveillance video and commercially available geospatial (mobile device) data generated at CTCL grant-funded drop box locations during the time periods in which drop boxes were in use for the 2020 General Election."

The work of True the Vote and their consultants is bringing into focus David Clements' vote trafficking parable[96] delivered at Mike Lindell's Cyber Symposium.

Did Ballot Traffickers Work in Minnesota?

If Minnesota was going to be comfortably won by Biden, it stands to reason that ballot traffickers would not need to be called into action in large numbers.

But many now understand that Minnesota may well have voted in favor of President Trump on November 3rd, 2020 (and possibly in

---

[94] https://www.truethevote.org/wp-content/uploads/2022/03/FILE_5193_no-meta.pdf
[95] https://www.truethevote.org/election-integrity-testimony-in-wisconsin-on-thursday-march-24-2022/
[96] https://rumble.com/vl2qbo-mike-lindell-cyber-symposium-professor-david-clements-the-vote-trafficking-.html

2016, too). A simple vote trend analysis of counties like Blue Earth[97] begins to raise questions and noticing the vote trend similarities across multiple counties[98] begs further inquiry.

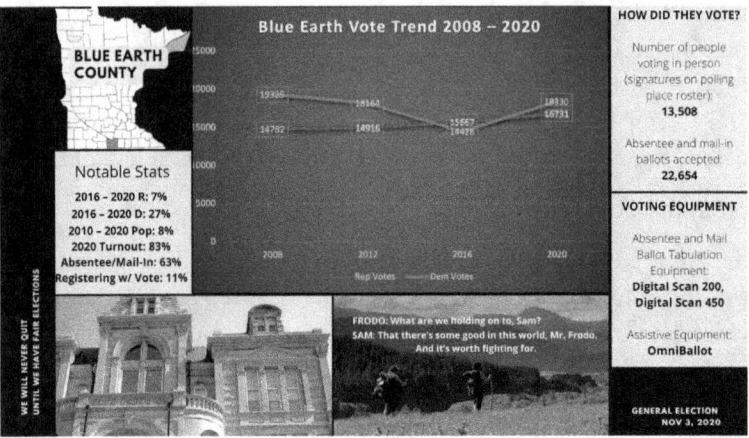

Blue Earth vote trend - https://www.youtube.com/watch?v=Wy5WJgyNtBQ

Captain Seth Keshel's trends[99], lawn signs, and word on the street in 2020 suggested it would be a close call and Minnesota Attorney General Keith Ellison even seemed worried based upon his 3:57pm tweet on election day: "...We don't have all the votes we need quite yet. So, help a friend (even a brand new friend) vote. Right now would be awesome." Was this a signal to unleash additional mules? Or could it be—to name just one more possibility—that the epollbook system notes which voters do not vote (neither submitting an absentee/mail-in vote nor voting in person in the precinct) and adds those voters to the phantom voter pile?

[97] https://www.youtube.com/watch?v=Wy5WJgyNtBQ
[98] https://www.youtube.com/playlist?list=PLCG2E0xbfHuBdl9DTuxkHRuvgxvO7vfjw
[99] https://rumble.com/vkf6t5-minnesota-election-audit-debrief-captain-seth-keshel.html

> **Keith Ellison**
> @keithellison
>
> If you've voted, great! Can you please call a friend? Spend a little time getting friends, fams, and folks out to the polls. We don't have all of the votes we need quite yet. So, help a friend (even a brand new friend) vote. Right now would be awesome.
>
> 3:57 PM · Nov 3, 2020 · Twitter for iPhone
>
> **188** Retweets   **876** Quote Tweets   **952** Likes

Could Ellison have had access to the SVRS in real-time on election day?

Therefore do not let Biden's official (unofficial) 7.2% margin deceive you; would Trump really have spent as much time and money here if Minnesota's 10 electoral college votes were not in play?

Now, many Minnesotans are aware their state is well known for daycare fraud and food fraud. It is emerging that voter, ballot, and election fraud are probably as prevalent, or worse, as indicated by a combination of trends, forensic analysis of Dominion systems also used in several Minnesota counties, and coordinated vote trafficking findings presented by True the Vote in the informational hearing before the Assembly Committee on Campaigns and Elections on March 24th, 2022 in Madison.

Even though Milwaukee officials failed to provide the requested video surveillance, geospatial data and cell phone signal data revealed vote or ballot trafficking into drop boxes to the tune of 137,000 ballots, or 7% of all WI ballots (in the sample, 138 people met a minimum threshold of visiting 5 NGOs and 25 drop boxes during the 2020 general election period, and 10% of that group were also present at a violent riot).

Is there any reason to believe organized ballot abuse isn't happening a few hundred miles west here in Minnesota? (In the cab ride to the Crystal Lake VFW for the CD5 Show[100] on Saturday April 2, 2022, the driver said he'd heard ballot harvesting and possible trafficking was happening in Minneapolis—word of mouth has long been effective but is especially powerful in our censorship-ridden world.)

Nationwide, about 160 million votes were apparently cast after experts predicted about 145 million would be. About 45% of the 160 million were absentee or mail-in ballots. In Minnesota, absentee or mail-in ballots represented 58% of the total reported votes by the secretary of state. In Minnesota, we have mail-in counties which speaks to the variance with nationwide numbers, but Minnesota's record absentee numbers may also suggest the success of the absentee voting marketing campaigns and influence operations.

The scale of absentee or mail-in ballots in Minnesota was immense. Over 1.9 million votes were apparently cast this way. That's a more than 1.2 million increase over the previous record.

Not only could absentee ballots sent to phantom voters that came back return-to-sender be collected, but NGOs may have had the ability to print ballots en masse and use mules to deliver them.

The rate at which canvassing in 30 Minnesota counties has shown that voters who reported voting in person were recorded as voting absentee raises questions.

The fact that more than 700,000 reported absentee votes were not connected to a voter in the statewide voter registration system (SVRS) 25 days after the election and only 5 days after the MN State Canvassing Board certified the election raises further questions.

Could it be that some percentage of these 700,000 reported absentee votes were coordinated by bad actors and therefore were not easily reconcilable in the electronic systems? For emphasis: 25 days after the election and 5 days after certification by the MN State Canvassing Board the numbers did not check out. And not by a

---

[100]https://erikvanmechelen.substack.com/p/the-cd5-show

little bit. By over 700,000.

The reasons for this remains an unresolved issue.

The following table with data from Rick Weible[101] shows the absentee ballots not connected by November 29th, 2020, in the MN SOS data in the Twin Cities area. Note that this work should be done immediately according to Minnesota Statute 203B.121 BALLOT BOARDS[102].

County	Absentee Ballots Not Connected
Anoka	4,537
Hennepin	17,830
Carver	33,741
Scott	46,220
Dakota	154,756
Ramsey	8,350
Washington	81,414

This is not an exhaustive list.

Furthermore, there is data gap between October 30 and November 3 which makes it difficult to audit the "must immediately" clause. The next table shows the absentee data and how it changed over time on the secretary of state's website.

Date Requested	Quantity	Date Accepted	Quantity
10/25/2020	1,765,327	10/23/2020	1,186,522
11/01/2020	1,969,728	10/30/2020	1,581,193
11/04/2020	2,129,804	11/03/2020	1,846,668
12/01/2020	2,129,804	11/03/2020	1,846,668
1/16/2021	2,193,411	1/14/2021	1,909,701
2/14/2021	2,193,411	1/14/2021	1,909,701

I've watched the room as Rick Weible has presented this data around the state. Many understand and are deeply concerned. They

---

[101] https://midwestswampwatch.com
[102] https://www.revisor.mn.gov/statutes/cite/203B.121

expect better from government especially when the issue concerns the sanctity of the elective franchise.

Minnesotans want to know whether their vote counted, whether it was cancelled out by a phantom vote, and whether a machine altered their vote.

On this last point, we turn to next in the Backup Attack Phase.

One of my friends recently asked me why a ground game as seen in 2000 Mules was needed if forensic audits can be denied and votes can be injected electronically. My simple response here is that the enemy would have preferred we not learn about the depth of cheating available through the machines. The illusions we are under need to be plausible enough, else our instincts to spot a lie kick in.

In other words, if you can cheat enough to win by inflating voter rolls and by stuffing the ballot box, you can potentially reduce the chances that people will ask questions about the machines in the first place. And those who control the machines, control who wins. Better to keep this reality under wraps.

This is part of the reason, I think, that while Hillary said she thought there was fraud in 2016, she may not have wanted to call for any audits. And history shows that she did not.

Chapter Three - Backup Attack

"The election of 2020 was not counted, it was calculated."

—Draza Smith, mathmetician

Draza Smith, Mark Cook, and Col. Shawn Smith

If the Attack Phase fails, the Backup Attack Phase comes into play.

This is where the story takes an interesting turn which may shake your previous understanding of how elections work.

For all the years of my life until 2020, I thought my vote counted. Then, in late 2020, I realized it probably didn't, but I didn't know how exactly.

Then, sometime in 2021, my perspective drastically (Drazatically) changed when I was introduced to Draza Smith's work and later met her at the Cyber Symposium. David Clements has described her as an "unsung hero".

What changed how I viewed elections?

Draza put it well: "The election of 2020 was not counted, it was calculated."

Start with an electoral college map of the United States. To win the presidential election takes 270 electoral college votes. Then, use a PID controller to generate outcomes at the state level in such a way that the desired candidate wins.

Easier said than done, because you don't know how many voters will turn out, either for the desired candidate or for the undesired candidate.

It's possible that the original set point in each state might need to be adjusted to get the desired outcome. Is this why vote counting needed to suddenly stop in multiple states in the middle of the night?

This part of the book, more than others, requires the visuals, charts, and graphs to be in front of you. If you are listening to the audiobook, print out the pages from the e-book freely available at https://leanpub.com/sim2020[103].

Edison Zero

For background on Edison data, recall this chart from Russ Ramsland's Georgia presentation in December 2020.

---

[103] https://leanpub.com/sim2020

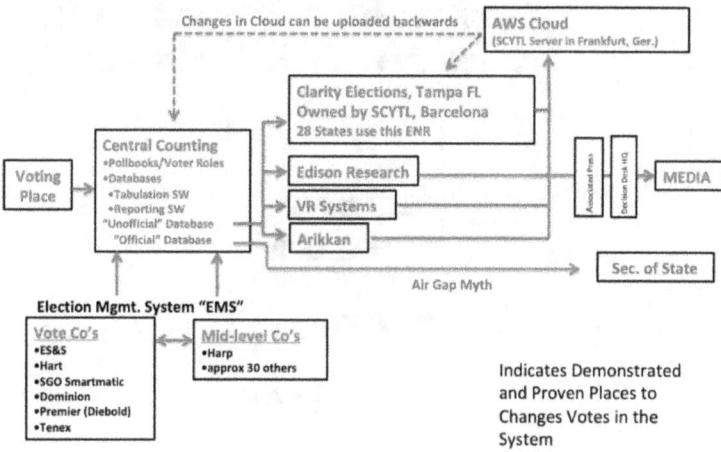

Edison receives data from "Unofficial Database"

Draza also writes: "For those asking - the Edison data reports the cumulative votes and the percentage that each candidate has during the election. But - during the Nov 2020 election, these reporting values all went through a rolling zero that then returned to relatively the same values on the next reporting cycle. It happened in series to each state and DC. I suspect that this was application of new setpoints and/or new control constants to drive the vote totals to the setpoint within the number of votes remaining in the count."

Here's an example of New Jersey's Edison Zero on November 4, 20202 starting at 4:01:23 AM and lasting until 11:35:48 AM.

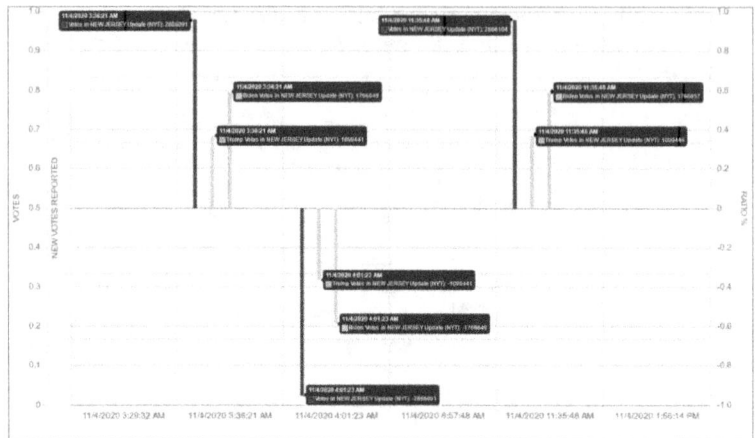

New Jersey's Edison Zero

Rhode Island

Erin Clements recommended I have a look at Draza's analysis of the Rhode Island cast vote record (CVR) and compare it with what Edison played on TV. Reason being that it was the "best synopsis of the set point phenomenon and the shuffle because that's the only place where we have apples to apples comparison between what we were told was happening on election night and what's actually stored inside the computer system—they can't be reconciled."

On Draza Smith's Telegram channel[104], all of the following charts and descriptions can be found by using the search function and typing "Rhode Island".

On August 3, 2021 Draza said: "So - Rhode Island is one of the more surprising plots I have seen so far. During the entire election reporting, the ratio of votes was on the Trump side of the line...until they were slammed down into their setpoint...

---

[104] https://t.me/ladydraza

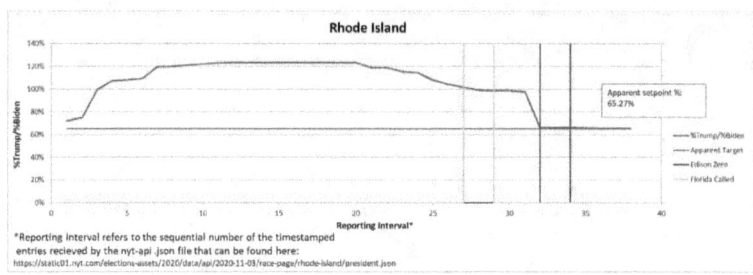

Rhode Island Edison Data

"Looking at the total vote trend, there was a clear preference, until that pesky Edison zero reset…."

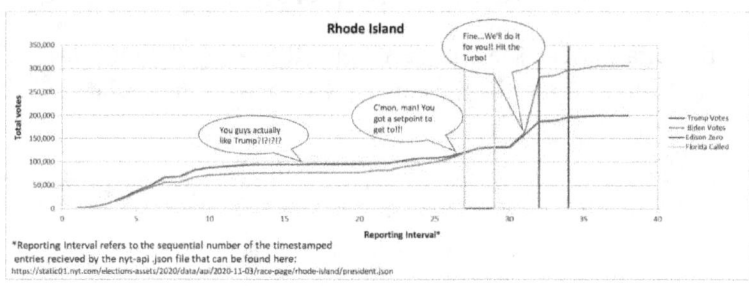

Set Point Reset

"From the Edison reported percentages, you can see the HUGE spike in the Biden votes prior to the reset, which has been indicative of receiving a new setpoint and higher tuning constants."

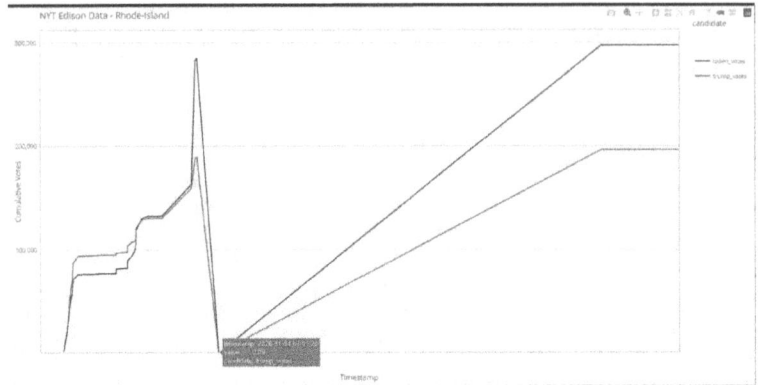

Spike in Biden votes prior to reset

"In the data you can see it happen here. The ratio setpoint is driven from 97% to 66% and the Edison zero happens 4 minutes later."

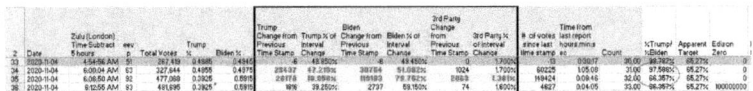

Setpoint Driven from 97% to 66%

Then, on the 21st of May, 2022, Draza announced this:

"I am so grateful our smallest state today. Because the entire state is smaller than many counties in other states, they do things a little more efficiently there, including counting all of their statewide votes with a single system that produces a STATEWIDE CVR.

"So, I have been saying for a while now that I have been confused about the fact that none of our counties/precincts can give a good explanation of how Edison and Scytl and SP are getting the election data to the NYT, etc. for election night reporting and CALLING THE RACES ON!

"But, I believe these companies know the playbook and just provide a probabilistic model to the viewers at home - so how can you question the results? You watched them come in live on TV! All the while the mules and machines and NGO's with electronic access to the voter rolls/poll books are working magic on the real votes have them end in the same place."

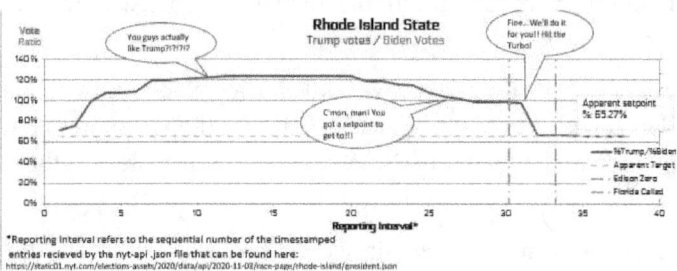

Trump to Biden ratio on election night

"So, here is the results as we saw them election night for the State of Rhode Island! This is how the ratio of Trump to Biden votes were reported by the news to all of us sitting at home on election night.

"That Drop towards Biden looks a little funny right there after FL was called for Trump, doesn't it?"

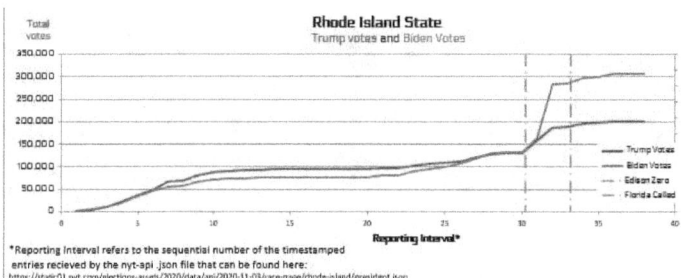

Trump and Biden votes on election night

"Here are the actual votes for each candidate that were reported over time. Did you realize little Rhode Island had their very own "F curve"?

"Well, actually it looks kind of like a snake in the grass..."

"So - now we have the CVR data to see what the MACHINE says about how the votes counted up. Before I show the plot, remember what we have learned through the work by Jeff O'Donnell on finding the two sets of books in the database. And my theory that they reshuffle the database to push those muled in votes that come in just under the wire forward in time to make it look like they were always there.

"This produces a distinctive curve with a drop and then a scoop (which Dr. D has termed the "Biden Boost" and then the votes float back upwards to the final setpoint, with corrections here and there. Right?

"Well, even here in RI where it would be totally obvious, the machines could not help themselves. It is in their code."

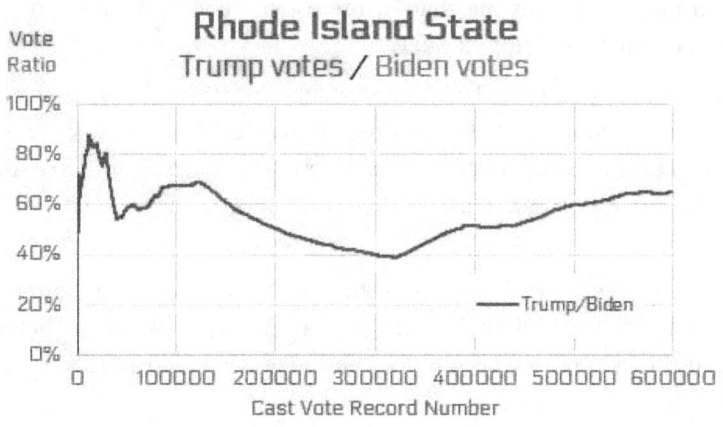

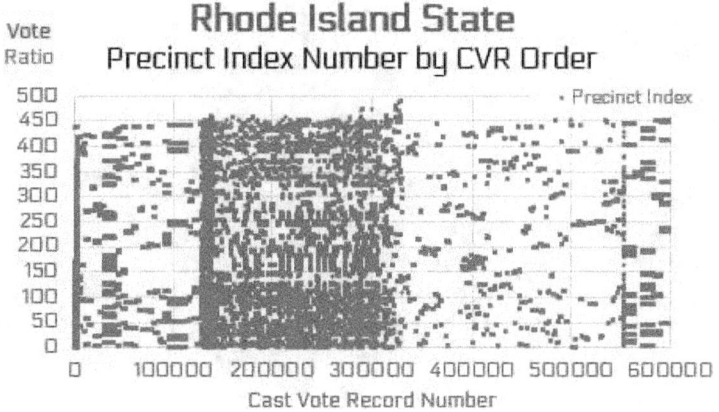

Rhode Island - How the votes actually came in

"So - here is what the machine told us with the CVR report of how the ratio of votes ACTUALLY *cough, cough* came in for Rhode Island over time.

"The blue graph below shows the precinct index that each ballot came in from. This is term I have developed for places that do not have numbered precincts. I take the list of precincts and record the precincts in order as they show up as precincts 1,2,3... and then I can plot them. Anyone that is interested - I can provide you my precinct name-to-number key.

"But what is notable here is - just like in other places, ALL the precincts report in at the very beginning (REPRESENT!) and then are shuffled to look almost too perfectly randomized with keeping some from every precinct in the back pocket to add at the end of counting.

"But - remember - if we were getting in votes perfectly randomized from all over the state - would the Law of Large Numbers dictate that this rollercoaster would be the shape we would expect?"

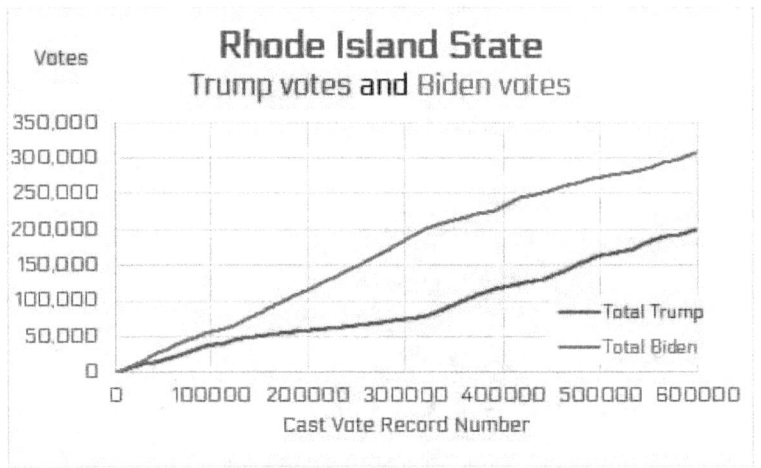

Trump and Biden votes in CVR

"And - if you could possible believe it, just look how evenly over time the votes came in for each candidate!! No snakes in the grass here…just in the programmers' seats."

"And - believe it or not - those RI Patriots collected more data - interim reports of vote counts, etc. NOTHING MATCHES, not the news data, to the machine data to the SecState data - sure , they all end up in the same place after a month or 2 of making 'corrections'."

2020-11-06	9:48:51 PM	505,201
2020-11-10	1:03:07 PM	513,323
2020-11-10	11:02:51 PM	513,411
2020-11-10	11:02:58 PM	513,503
2020-11-13	9:51:01 PM	513,602
2020-11-24	7:40:55 PM	513,627
2020-11-25	4:38:09 AM	517,757
2020-12-11	4:15:51 PM	514,238
2020-12-11	4:20:36 PM	516,434
2020-12-11	4:23:58 PM	517,757
2020-12-11	4:23:58 PM	517,757

Edison corrections

"Check out the corrections that the Edison data made to get to the final results - after over a month worth of "corrections and updates" - because this is how we should count election votes.

"P.S: I dropped out the reported vote from the AP that wasn't Edison because they appear to not have ben synchronized and make even more crazy jumps, as a result."

Minnesota's Simulation

No Minnesotan has been given any cast vote records from their county and it is hard to say whether any counties actually have them, for various reasons. Not being able to produce an audit trail of the machine count, when the machine count is the primary method of counting, is unacceptable.

Since we do not have the cast vote records from any county, let alone the entire state as Rhode Island was able to produce, let's make do with what we can.

Let's start take a look at how votes were reported to the media (refer back to Russ Ramsland's slide above for reference). The following graphic shows how the votes were sent through to the media from Edison Research. Notice the negative 194,846 votes near interval 50.

In a system that is aggregating votes, should there ever be a drop in nearly 200,000 votes? What may have caused that?

Here again I will quote Draza Smith:

"So - Minnesota had some really interesting things going on that took a little bit of thought. I am finding a lot of events that happen across states that help me try to convince all of you our elections are completely controlled events. Minnesota - I believe - kinda went like this:"

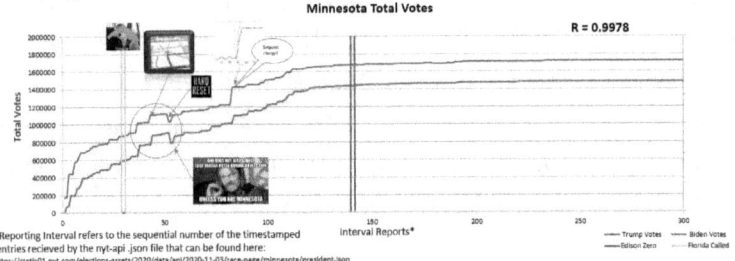

Minnesota Total Votes

"The overall votes have a very high correlation with an R value of 0.9978, which is higher than Pennsylvania, but Pennsylvania was the states that had the same "event" happen, with regard to the loss of votes during counting. I pulled up the similar curve from Pennsylvania and, not only is the shape factor almost exactly the same, but it happened during almost the same counting interval number - around 50 - which, timewise, was shortly after the Florida surprise."

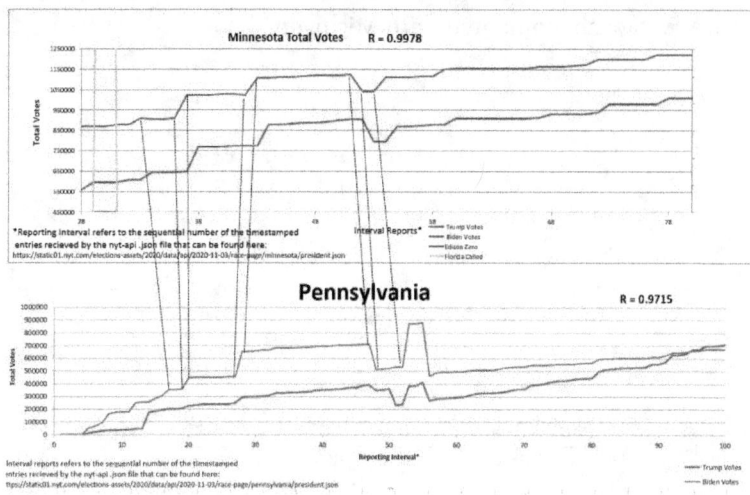

Comparing MN to PA

"The difference in the shape that follows whatever was happening that caused the similarity between the events in PA and MN is the result of the difference in the initial perturbation that was assigned to each state. PA had one that was more chaotic that MN."

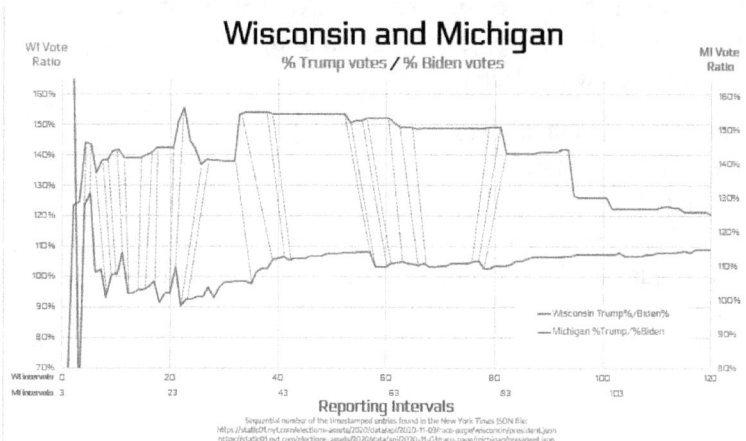

Wisconsin and Michigan - %Trump Votes/%Biden Votes

To demonstrate that similarites between states are not isolated, notice Wisconsin compared with Michigan.

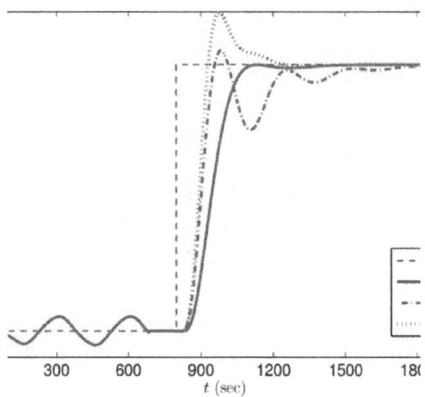

Setpoint Input Process

"The "setpoint change" that appears to occur later on is most likely the result of a slight shifting in position as MI was being moved in the lineup. I refer to this as a setpoint change, because it bears a striking resemblance to what we would see in any industrial system that is being controlled and experiences a setpoint change. This is the image that I used on the graph above that - should - have nothing to do with elections."

When Draza refers to MI (Michigan) being moved in the lineup, consider that since Florida's Trump turnout was so high the algorithm was not going to be set in such a way to achieve a Biden win. It appears the decision was made by the powers that be to let Trump win Florida but pick up those electoral college votes elsewhere. Thus Michigan being moved in the lineup.

National Key for Setpoints

"If we go back and look at the national key calculated from the final values, you can see that MN is right there at the edge of the shuffle - and probably was affected by the moving of MI into the Biden side of the curve."

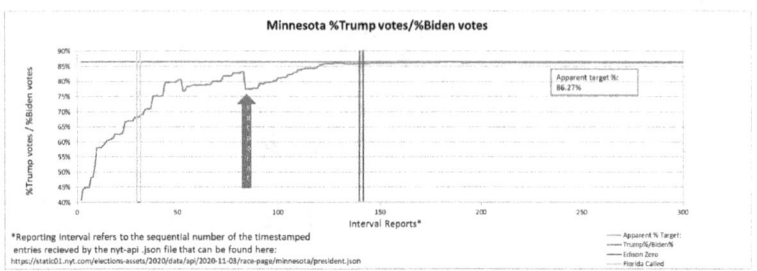

Ratio of Trump to Biden votes

"Here you can see the ratio control curve with a bit of a chaotic start and that "event" after Florida was called. But, after she got her final setpoint, the curve just eased its way into the final setpoint, like we have seen in so many other states."

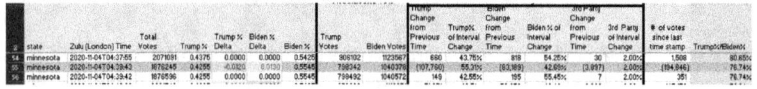

Adjustment to final setpoint

"Now, the adjustment to that final setpoint was really a herculean effort by our vote counters. We were able to report 289157 votes in 17 seconds. This reduced the percentage from 83% to 77% Trump to Biden votes, because Biden received the lion's share of that valiant effort."

194,846 vote reduction

"So - that number - 194846 - is kinda like the other reductions we have seen in other states. If you take that number and divide it by the total on the line above, it is usually apparent that is it a calculated reduction. If we do that here 194846/2071091 = 9.41% reduction. I would have expected it to be 9.5% of 10%...a nice round reduction like seen in other states. So, I looked as what we have going on. If we look at the reduction in just Trump's votes, what we have on this line is a reduction coupled with a flip from the 3rd party. If we remove the flip from the 3rd party, we get a reduction of 87049.15 votes from Trump's tally, which is a 4.20% reduction in Trump's overall vote at that time."

Cleanup reductions

"Annnddd - we finish up, much like the other states. We have our percentage control of the interval hanging tight - while we find places for the reductions to happen, without changing either the interval percentage distribution or the overall percentage ratio. These cleanup reductions are in between the reports that take about 10 minutes for each single vote to be counted. I guess they were tired from the big push earlier."

Does reviewing this data make you look at our election process differently?

I know when I first saw this data about nine months ago I was unsettled—I hadn't considered this possibility. But with this new information I went forth with new questions. (See chapter 10 for a brief history of voting machines.)

Remember that the Backup Attack phase is used when the initial attack doesn't go as planned. The biggest tool is the injection of votes electronically. If this can be done without detection, a race can still be won regardless of how many physical ballots were delivered absentee (dropbox or mail-in) or at the in-person polling place on election day and subsequently scanned through tabulators. In a totalitarian system, election night reporting could be largely or actual theater and disconnected from results aggregated at lower levels; citizens could be shown results and then later barred from auditing election materials altogether.

There is a theory out there which Draza's data begins to provide evidence for that the 2020 election was less an election and more a simulation disguised as an election. (This is in part why I made the acronym for the title of this book = SIM.) We don't *need* that perspective to lay out the anomalies, indicators, and evidence we've done up to this point in the book, but it does serve to provide a working explanation for the irregularities reported around the state and in the Edison Research data. Data is only as good as its source.

Once the simulation concept is understood, lower level manipulation can occur in the databases or voting machines in counties and precincts to achieve results at that lower level which align with the top-down algorithms.

Case in point: Around September 2021, I remember video calls where Jeffrey O'Donnell and Dan Sundin shared preliminary findings from the before and after server images revealed by Tina Peters on Days 1 and 2 of Lindell's Cyber Symposium (see the documentary Selection Code[105] for more details). To this day I encounter folks who were disappointed by the event in Sioux Falls: I may share their confusion regarding the PCAPs but I will not hesitate to point them to Jeffrey O'Donnell's Mesa Report #3[106], which showed "unauthorized creation of new election databases during early voting in the 2020 General Election on October 21, 2020, followed by the digital reloading of 20,346 ballot records into the new election databases, making the original voter intent recorded from the ballots unknown." Furthermore, "5,567 ballots in 58 batches did not have their digital records copied to the new

---

[105]https://selectioncode.com
[106]https://magaraccoon.com/docs/MesaCountyReport3.pdf

database, although the votes from the ballots in those batches were recorded in the Main election database."

This was only the first of seven major findings and implications. For any states using Dominion Voting Systems (DVS) Election Management System (EMS), this should be concerning. An audit of the machines would demonstrate that this did not occur in the six counties in Minnesota also using Dominion systems. Until that happens, how can voters be confident something like this didn't happen in Minnesota?

If the cover up in the Defense Phase, which we turn to next, is good enough, then many citizens will not immediately be able to find out exactly how subversion of their elections took place.

Chapter Four - Defense

"Since we know what we will find when we do our audits—"

"That we've been duped."

"Yes, so what's stopping us from reformulating our election processes as you described earlier and then immediately calling for new elections?"

"Nothing."

—From a conversation between Col. Phil Waldren and the author inside The Military Heritage Alliance around 6pm on Day Three of Mike Lindell's Cyber Symposium in Sioux Falls, South Dakota on August 12, 2021

The Defense Phase is where the attackers try to defend against what Patrick Colbeck calls the meddling kids from discovering what they did. It involves cover ups, destruction of physical and digitial evidence (Dominion's Trusted Build), slow walking and infiltration of livestreamed election audits (the Maricopa audit), media bullying, and lawfare.

This phase began on election night 2020 (and before that) and it is where we are in June 2022 as this book goes to the press.

Some object to the prospect of coordinated fraud on the grounds that it would not be so easy to cover up.

But if there were people smart enough, sophisticated enough, and resourceful enough to pull off such a heist nationally (and likely involving international components), don't you think they would have some kind of plan to get away with it? They did, although in retrospect it was a bit sloppy. And fortunately there were eyes on their actions. People like Patrick Colbeck, author of *The 2020 Coup*, were on the scene at the TCF center in Detroit serving as a certified Poll Challenger. And people like Jeffrey O'Donnell and so many others have joined the fight since.

The people that did this may be clever, but it was an uphill task to pull every lever and not spring a leak.

The first leak was on election night when there was a coordinated pause to vote counting[107] in multiple states.

That alerted millions if not tens of millions to the coup right from the start. It was only a matter of time before the riddle could be solved, despite extensive interference from many you might have thought would have supported election accuracy and transparency, but who have revealed that they do not.

Part of Their Plan?

At the Cyber Symposium, Dr. Shiva gave a presentation which detailed the connections between the various players and mentioned a few of their published playbooks. One of these was The Long Fuse[108], by the Election Integrity Partnership.

On page 3, the 'Data Cleanup' phase immediately follows the election. What data exactly needed to be cleaned up?

---

[107] https://www.mixonium.com/public/post/11555
[108] https://projectapario.com/Browse?document=WJT9LCRAJ&filename=EIP-Final-Report.pdf

1.2. The EIP: Partner Organizations and Structure

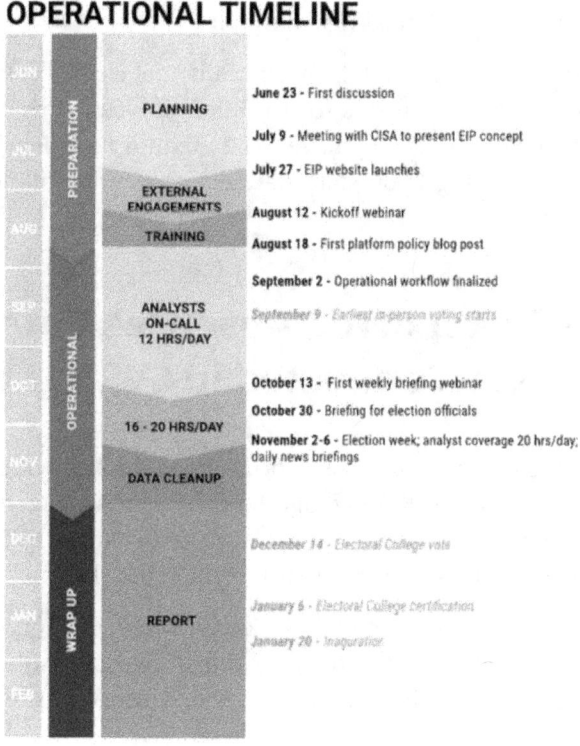

Figure 1.1: Timeline of the Election Integrity Partnership's work.

Part of the plan

Part of the data cleanup being done would need to happen with the voter rolls. Public requests of these rolls and comparisons between them show large changes across time in registrations. Presumably this could cover up large additions of phantom voters just prior to elections.

But what is harder to cover up is detailed comparisons across counties in a single state, as was shown by Erin Clements in New Mexico's voter rolls, or the proof of database manipulation in the Mesa County, Colorado Dominion Trusted Build.

Here's Hoang Quan on the Trusted Build:

Which by the way should be technically deficient, because it invalidates the 22-month rule for retention of election records. If you can't audit, review, why have the 22-month retention period (or longer, depending upon state statutes of retention of election records).

700,000 Reported Absentee Voters Not Connected in SVRS

Rick Weible's database analysis[109] of Minnesota's statewide voter registration system (SVRS) highlighted that there were more than 700,000 absentee voters reported than documented in the SVRS five days *after* the MN Canvassing Board certified the election.

In a June 7, 2022 GGP meeting in Dakota County, election official Andy Lokken said that after the fact comparative analysis of SOS-reported data with the SVRS data was not an effective way to verify results.

Then how *should* an election be verified by the people?

Bear in mind that no statewide nor any county-wide full forensic audits (of all election materials, not a recount of ballots) has been done in Minnesota. Citizens have faced considerable resistance from those responsible for ensuring that no voter is disenfranchised and have succeeded in finding numerous indicators and proof that election processes were not followed according to statute and that the results are therefore seriously in question.

---

[109] https://midwestswampwatch.com

Regarding the absentee voters: If the SOS data was not at all consistent with the SVRS data 25 days *after* the November 3, 2020 election, *when* was it going to be? And how did the MN State Canvassing Board certify the election 5 days prior with such a large discrepancy? To repeat, on November 29, 2020, just 5 days after the MN Canvassing Board certified the election, more than 700,000 reported absentee voters were not connected in the statewide voter registration system.

This fact alone should have triggered a statewide audit and uproar from any elected officials that care about election integrity. If you are unsure about your local elected officials, ask them what they think about this issue and whether they believe we ought to have higher standards for our absentee ballot process as it pertains to data accuracy in our statewide voter registration system.

From the perspective of the defense phase relating to absentee ballot coverup, deflection and obfuscation of this fact (it still remains unresolved) should be expected—the general public learning this certainly threatens to undermine the credibility of those at the helm.

Minnesota Post Election Review Reveals Missing Ballots

The local media likes to report on the success of risk-limiting audits (RLAs), recounts, and post-election reviews. Let's discuss why these are not suitable to demonstrate the total accuracy and integrity of a machine-driven election.

In Minnesota only about 3% of of precincts per county are subject to a post-election review according to Minnesota Statute 206.89 POSTELECTION REVIEW OF VOTING SYSTEMS[110].

---

[110] https://www.revisor.mn.gov/statutes/cite/206.89

A post election review[111] hand counts ballots returned by the optical scan ballot counters in select precincts. (These are sometimes referred to as risk-limiting audits, although how much risk do they truly mitigate?)

Precinct: 4950 - WEST ST PAUL W-2 P-2						Dakota County
Office: U.S. President & Vice President						
Candidate Name	Total Votes	Total Hand-Counted Votes	Total Unadjusted Difference *	Total Explained Difference	Total Adjusted Difference	Explanation
Donald J. Trump and Michael R. Pence	376	193	185	1	0	PP: voter intent
Joseph R. Biden and Kamala Harris	912	247	689	2	0	PP: voter intent
Roque "Rocky" De La Fuente and Darcy Richardson	1	1	0	0	0	
Howie Hawkins and Angela Walker	1	1	0	0	0	
Kanye West and Michelle Tidball	3	1	2	0	0	
Brock Pierce and Karla Ballard	4	2	2	0	0	
Gloria La Riva and Leonard Peltier	2	1	1	0	0	
Alyson Kennedy and Malcolm Jarrett	0	0	0	0	0	
Jo Jorgensen and Jeremy "Spike" Cohen	10	8	2	0	0	
BLANK FOR OFFICE	4	5	1	1	0	PP: voter intent
OVER / DEFECTIVE FOR OFFICE	7	4	3	3	0	PP: voter intent
WRITE-IN**	7	2	5	0	0	
Totals	1327	465	870	7	0	
Final Results			Difference of not more than 0.5%		0%	ACCEPTABLE

* Total Unadjusted Difference is the sum of Unadjusted Difference for polling place votes and Unadjusted Difference for absentee/mail ballot votes. It will not always equal the difference between Total Votes and Total Hand Counted Votes.

863 votes not explained but considered ACCEPTABLE

In a postelection review in Dakota County's Precinct 4950, WEST ST PAUL W-2 P-2, the total unadjusted difference was 870 votes. 7 of those 870 votes were explained, but 863 were not explained. Why then does the total adjusted difference (the last column) show all zeros? The total adjusted difference should read 863 (870 minus 7). Even with 65% (863 out of 1327) of the total votes in this postelection review left unexplained, the Final Results row says this is a "Difference of not more than 0.5%" and the Total Adjusted Difference is "0%", deemed "ACCEPTABLE".

Of course, this is clearly **not** acceptable and it begs the question: How many more precincts would turn up red flags like this if more postelection reviews had been done? And how many more red flags might be raised if proper audits were done? Is this why cast vote records (CVRs) have not been forthcoming from local election officials? With this work being shown to Minnesotans, it would be

---

[111] https://www.sos.state.mn.us/elections-voting/how-elections-work/post-election-reviews/

strange if they were not asking for audits and accountability.

What this example demonstrates even more is the difficulty of reconciling the paper ballots to the machine counts. If a top-down simulation is being run that needs to be backfilled after the fact with ballot (or printer) deliveries to precincts and counties 2000-Mules style, but that last-minute work isn't completed, then the outcome would be what we've seen in Dakota County's Precinct 4950.

What's more, by comparing the increases to Trump votes (from hand count to total votes) with the increases to Biden votes (from hand count to total votes), we also gain insight into how an weighted ratio algorithm might have been used to increase Biden votes by almost 269% while Trump votes only increased by 95%.

You be the judge. Was this data cleaned up well?

When Kim Bauer received in June 2022 the receipts from post-election reviews done in Dakota County for 2020 as well as 2021 (when her school board election took place), it was discovered that some of the post-election review documentation differed from the originals.

A Petition to Stop the Certification of Minnesota's Election

Based on the postelection review above (but not only that) it was correct for Susan Shogren Smith[112] to properly serve a petition[113] to each member of the Minnesota State Canvassing Board prior to its certification of the 2020 election, in part reading:

"Minnesota candidates for office and voters have come forward with affadavits detailing concerns and observations about the ignored and failed election processes in counties across the state...If

---

[112]https://shogrensmithlaw.com/about-us
[113]https://erikvanmechelen.substack.com/p/should-minnesotas-2020-election-have

this Court does not take action to prevent the certification of the Minnesota election until a complete, bi-partisan statewide audit of the election occurs, including election materials, our election system, and the trust of the voters, will be irreparably harmed."

The MN State Canvassing Board is the sole entity identified in the MN Constitution carrying the duty to canvass the statewide election results. However, the MN Supreme Court erroneously ruled (in my opinion) that all 87 counties had to be served. Therefore the case was dismissed[114] without a hearing on the facts on Friday afternoon, December 4, 2020. This dismissal was critical to meeting the the safe harbor deadline of December 8, 2020.

Since that time, every point made in the petition has been confirmed by the work of Rick Weible and others, including "issues related to procedure, observer and election judge access, voter intimidation, lost ballots, lost absentee envelopes, missing election materials and questionable ballots… [and] concerns about voting equipment transmitting results during the early counting period on election day."

---

[114] https://www.documentcloud.org/documents/20420161-order-minnesota-supreme-court-dismisses-gop-election-contest

Crow Wing County

Crow Wing Commissioners and County Attorney

After multiple commissioner board meetings attended by dozens of Minnesotans who didn't trust the results of the 2020 election, the commissioners were finally persuaded in late December to pass a resolution seeking an audit. Don Ryan, the County Attorney, interpreted Minnesota law and advised that the county could not unseal its own ballots, and so the request was made to Secretary of State Steve Simon, who declined to undertake a full forensic audit of all election material and data.

In their resolution, which passed 4-1, the commissioners stated that the board "continues to have faith in the 2020 election results as valid and reliable but it is equally troubling that there are citizens who still have a sincerely held belief that it was not", suggesting they did not wholeheartedly agree with their constituents and were perhaps going ahead with the resolution as a matter of appeasement. In May 2022, at least one of the same commissioners was afraid to open an email[115] with a link to 2000 Mules when

---

[115] https://www.youtube.com/watch?v=HC7E3qCA_3k

candidate for house rep Doug Kern sent it to the Board.

"Our office will not engage in a vague and impossibly broad search for unspecified misconduct based on anyone's gut feeling, hunch, or belief — no matter how sincerely held," Simon said. "The 2020 general election, which took place almost 15 months ago, was fundamentally fair, accurate, honest, and secure across Minnesota."

STATE OF MINNESOTA
Office of Minnesota Secretary of State
Steve Simon

January 31, 2022

Crow Wing County Board of County Commissioners
County Administrator's Office
Historic Courthouse
326 Laurel Street, Suite 13
Brainerd, MN 56401

Honorable Commissioners:

This is a response to the Crow Wing County Board resolution dated January 4, 2022 (received on January 25, 2022) requesting that the Office of Secretary of State "undertake a full forensic audit of all election material and data" related to the 2020 election in Crow Wing County.

We appreciate the delicate balancing act that you've attempted as you seek to address the concerns of some of your constituents. On the one hand, you've acknowledged that you continue "to have faith in the 2020 election results as valid and reliable." (Crow Wing County Attorney Don Ryan has said much the same thing.) On the other hand, you've recognized that some of your constituents hold sincerely held beliefs to the contrary.

Part of Minnesota's consistent election integrity stems from our outstanding local election administrators, including in Crow Wing County. Our local administrators do much of the hard work of running a successful election. To name only a few examples of their work, they purchase and test election equipment, they order ballots, they hire and train election judges, they run the absentee balloting process, they handle ballot security, and they count the votes. They do so in an ethical, principled, competent, and non-political way. Consistent with Minnesota law, Crow Wing County administrators already engaged in a thorough post-election audit and a post-election review after the 2020 general election – with results showing no irregularities and no cause to suspect misconduct. Our office has reviewed their work, and has found it to be professional, legal, and precise.

180 State Office Building | 100 Rev. Dr. Martin Luther King, Jr. Blvd. | Saint Paul, MN 55155-1299
Phone: 651-201-1324 or 1-877-600-8683 | Fax: 651-215-0682 | MN Relay Service: 711
E-mail: secretary.state@state.mn.us | Web site: www.sos.state.mn.us

Secretary of State Simon's response, page 1 of 2

> There is no legitimate reason to second-guess the integrity of the 2020 election in Crow Wing County. The county has already done its duty with great skill, and the system worked as it was designed – and as the public has every right to expect. Our office will not engage in a vague and impossibly broad search for unspecified misconduct (i.e. "a full forensic audit of all election material and data") based on anyone's gut feeling, hunch, or belief – no matter how sincerely held. For those who claim to have actual evidence of potential wrongdoing, the proper place to share that evidence is a law enforcement agency.
>
> The 2020 general election, which took place almost fifteen months ago, was fundamentally fair, accurate, honest, and secure across Minnesota. Nearly eighty percent of Minnesotans showed their confidence in our system by showing up to vote – making our state #1 in America in voter participation (for the third time in a row). We should all be proud of that. Other states envy our record.
>
> The administrative success of the 2020 election suggests that there's cause for continued optimism about democracy in Minnesota and in America. But in the short-term, we have serious challenges. The most dangerous challenge is the spread of disinformation about our election system. Too many people have been misled by the deceptions of those with a political or financial motive to corrode confidence in our democracy. Meanwhile, foreign adversaries not only cheer our disunity – but actively encourage it by helping to spread lies about our election system through multiple channels. It's all so poisonous, and it needs to stop. I believe it will stop – if enough of us stand up to it.
>
> I know you are doing your best to try to serve the public. Thanks for your service to Crow Wing County and to Minnesota. As always, I hope you'll feel free to let me know how our office can be a resource for you.
>
> Sincerely,
>
> *Steve Simon*
>
> Steve Simon
> Minnesota Secretary of State

Secretary of State Simon's response, page 2 of 2

If the Secretary of State *had* complied with the commissioners' request, election materials and machines may have been audited. This would have been a proper audit instead of a post election review or a recount which simply audits the *results*.

Why should the machines and data be audited? Because, as was shown by Jeff Lensburg in the Antrim County, Michigan case, votes can easily be swapped[116] which would not be identified in a canvass, postelection review, or risk-limiting audit (recount).

However, if the machines and full chain of custody—of both materials and data— were to be audited, the vulnerabilities described in earlier chapters could be exposed.

Secretary of State Steve Simon made this decision in January, 2022, missing an opportunity to demonstrate transparency in Minnesota's election process and systems.

Since then, an even faster method to verify whether the paper ballots match the machine count (as scanned through the tabulators) has been identified.

Dakota County

When the people with Rick Weible's help found indications that the results Dakota County announced for Kim Bauer's 2021 School Board race in ISD 196 may not have been accurate, they began requesting information from the county to try to reconcile the mismatching information.

To this day, the data in the statewide voter registration system and the reported results from the county and the reported results from the school district have not been reconciled.

In May I sat in a closed door meeting where the county election officials tried to explain what they thought happened but were unable to satisfyingly do so. This meeting in particular gave me insight into the depth of the problem we face, since it is my opinion that some election officials simply do not understand the technical details of the software and hardware, whereas others may very well understand but be held back from helping us by some as yet to be

---

[116]https://rumble.com/vgi89t-hacking-democracy-antrim-county-mi-edition.html

discovered reason. In that particular meeting also was the election official's boss, who tried to steer the meeting. He previously had said I could not record the county commissioner meetings, when of course I could (and did) seeing as they are open meetings.

On June 7, 2022, Rick Weible spoke to Dakota County about their software[117], recommending they return to hand counting and hand tallying.

That day, the county commissioners voted favorably on not approving drop box voting and returning to party balance on absentee ballot boards while Andy Lokken described Minnesota's unique situation[118], which is "so unique that it creates delays in getting software here."

There is more work to do since Dakota County (and every county in Minnesota) still uses the modern electronic voting systems which are highly vulnerable to subversion.

Wright County

The teams in Wright County were successful in convincing the county commissioners there to hold a workshop dedicated to election integrity[119] with Rick Weible as the speaker, on May 17, 2022.

At the close of this meeting, it was decided that a joint task force would be put in place involving county commissioners, election officials, and members of the public.

---

[117] https://rumble.com/v1998gh-rick-weible-informs-dakota-county-about-their-software.html
[118] https://youtu.be/mE1e3XGf7xM
[119] https://rumble.com/v157g8v-rick-weible-in-wright-county-may-17-2022.html

Morrison County

After Jeremy Pekula went on the radio asking whether the county commissioners were going to take action, he received another invitation to meet.

In mid May, after speaking on the radio alongside Jeremy in the morning, we met that afternoon with the County Administrator, two county commissioners, the head election official, and the deputy election official.

We shared some of the information already discussed in this book.

We asked whether they would like to have an item on the agenda in a forthcoming county commmissioners meeting.

So far they have not agreed to do so.

Sherburne County

Teri Dickinson was very effective in organizing people to attend county commissioner meetings in Sherburne County. She even once gave up her precious speaking slot to give me three minutes to anchor a slate of speakers including Kari Watkins, who that day shared details from the Halderman report. I stressed the opportunity for the commissioners to take in all the information and find it in themselves to make history by removing the machines.

The Sherburne county commissioners refused to (so far) have a public hearing or agenda item during the county commissioner board meeting despite multiple weeks of open forum comments like Rick Weible's here[120] sharing critical vulnerabilities with Sherburne's modern electronic voting equipment. This inability to listen or disinterest in the facts led Kari Watkins to step up and run for county commissioner herself.

---

[120]https://rumble.com/v15hs5h-voting-improvements-sherburne-county-may-3-2022.html

Because of this roadblock, the action teams pivoted to meetings with the townships.

A Haven Township meeting on June 20, 2022 started out with the usual disappointments and interference. Instead of Rick Weible's presentation starting the 7 p.m. meeting, as had been promised, he and those attending who had travelled to attend were made to wait until almost 9 p.m. once other items at the supervisor's meeting had been completed. Rick was then offered 10 minutes. After negotiation, he was given around 40 minutes, with the supervisor's interjecting with questions.

The meeting was then adjourned after the Chair said her eyes were glazing over, but three of the supervisor's stayed around to hear more of Rick's presentation, which went about another hour.

By the end, one of the supervisors said to me walking out of the building, "If we don't get to hand count here, I'm not going to certify the election," referring to the primary on August 9.

This was music to my ears.

Where Are the Cast Vote Records?

Cast vote records (CVR) allow the machines to tell on themselves. Without them, the machine audit trail is severely limited.

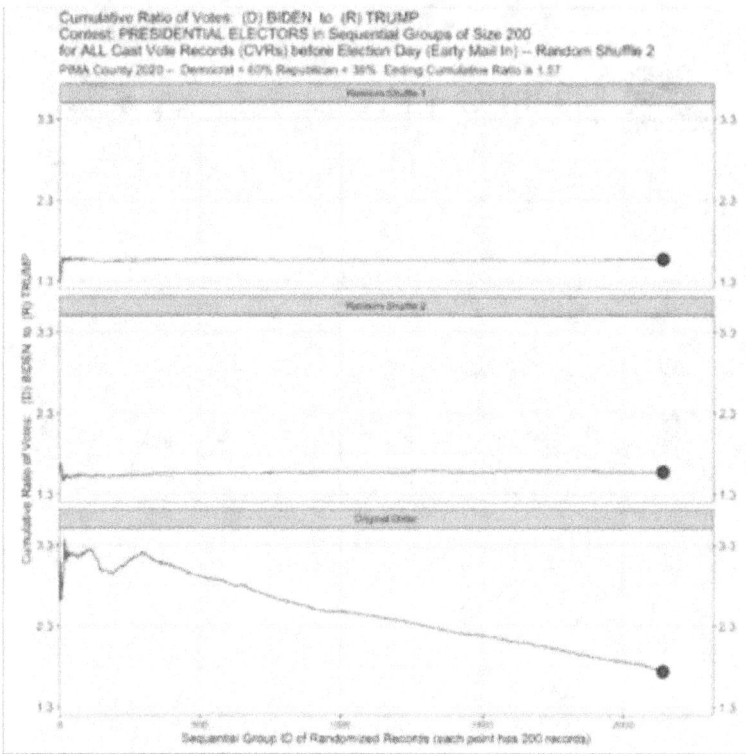

Pima County Cast Vote Records

Have a look at this CVR from Pima County.

The top two graphs look good.

But the third (bottom) CVR is not realistic. The only way that could happen is if there happened to be several thousand Biden ballots show up at the same time. Then you might see that driving toward the setpoint. But this graph clearly shows a defiance of the law of large numbers.

To date no CVR reports have been shared with the public despite numerous public data requests to county election officials and their offices throughout the state.

Here's just one response from the Todd County Attorney:

CHARLES G. RASMUSSEN
Todd County Attorney

Jane M. Gustafson
John E. Lindemann
Heidi E. Schultz
Christopher D. Mathews
Assistant County Attorneys

221 1st Avenue South, Suite 400, Long Prairie, MN 56347
Phone: 320-732-6039 Fax: 320-732-4120
toddcountyattorney@co.todd.mn.us

March 24, 2022

Denise Gaida
Auditor/Treasurer
Todd County Courthouse
Long Prairie, MN 56347

RE: Eric Van Mechelen Email Requests

Dear Denise:

I have reviewed the string of e-mails concerning Mr. Erik van Mechelen's request for CVR cast vote record reports for the November 2020 election. It is my understanding that Todd County does not create this data nor does it have such data stored anywhere. Chapter 13 does not require Todd County to create any data if it does not exist. Therefore, since Todd County does not have this data, it cannot comply with the request. Thank you.

Sincerely,

Charles G. Rasmussen
Todd County Attorney

/smp

"Todd County does not create this data"

But ES&S's own manuals describe the availability of this functionality.

Question 4

Risk Limiting Audits

Do you have a system in place for a post-election risk limiting audit, if so elaborate? Do you work with an outside vendor to accomplish your proposed post-election risk limiting audit? If you are not selected to provide voting systems to Allegheny County, would you have interest in performing post-election risk limiting audits?

ES&S IS A STRONG SUPPORTER OF POST-ELECTION AUDITS — A WAY FOR ELECTION OFFICIALS TO VERIFY VOTES WERE COUNTED ACCURATELY.

ES&S hardware and software have been designed to accommodate numerous methodologies for conducting a Risk Limiting Audits (RLAs). All proposed ES&S tabulation equipment creates a unique cast vote record (CVR), which identifies selections made by the voter. The CVR is the official count of the vote used for tallying of results in the ES&S software, called Electionware.

The Cast Voter Record and the corresponding digital image of the ballot are saved to the results media and transferred to Electionware upon uploading results. Electionware software allows the user to call up and review any vote cast during the election and compare the ballot image alongside the Cast Vote Record, enabling a manual count of the ballot to be performed alongside the machine's results.

A list of the Cast Vote Records can be exported from the software to provide a manifest useful for random selection of ballots to be audited. Other jurisdictions have used this list in conjunction with third party selection tools to determine the number of ballots to be audited, and to randomize the Cast Vote Record numbers to be audited based on total votes cast, margin of victory, and other various criteria for establishing the parameters of the Risk Limiting Audit. ES&S looks forward to the opportunity to consult on this matter and advise how the ES&S system has been used in numerous Risk Limiting Audits across the United States. We can also detail how other Pennsylvania jurisdictions (i.e. Philadelphia) intend to utilize the ES&S system for future audits.

CVR described by ES&S

I even sent the Todd County election officials a PDF of how to extract the CVRs, which are page 42 of the ES&S Electionware Volume V: Results User's Guide.

110   Chapter Four - Defense

Chapter 3: Produce Module   49

The following is a sample of a Cast Vote Record export file:

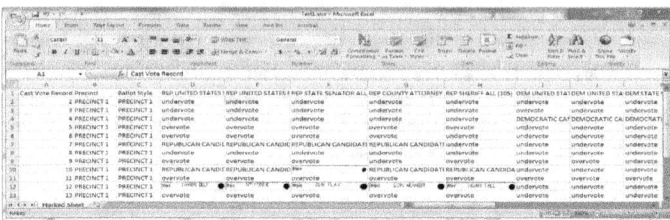

Sample Export of CVR

Chapter 3: Produce Module   47

Sample Cast Vote Record:

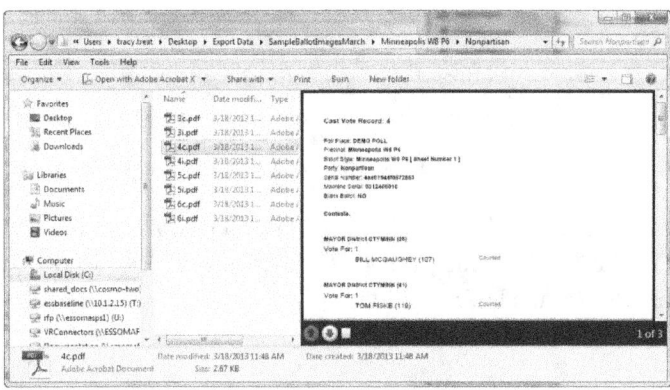

To export Cast Vote Records, and optionally write-in images:

The **Export Cast Vote Records** function exports cast vote record text for selected races, and optionally clippings of write-in selections from the ballots to an (.xls) file

1. Select **Export Cast Vote Records** from the **Tools** menu.

The Cast Vote Record Export window is displayed.

How to export the CVR

No response was given to the following email since I sent it on April

29, 2022.

[7] Public Records Request - Todd County Cast Vote Record (CVR) Report

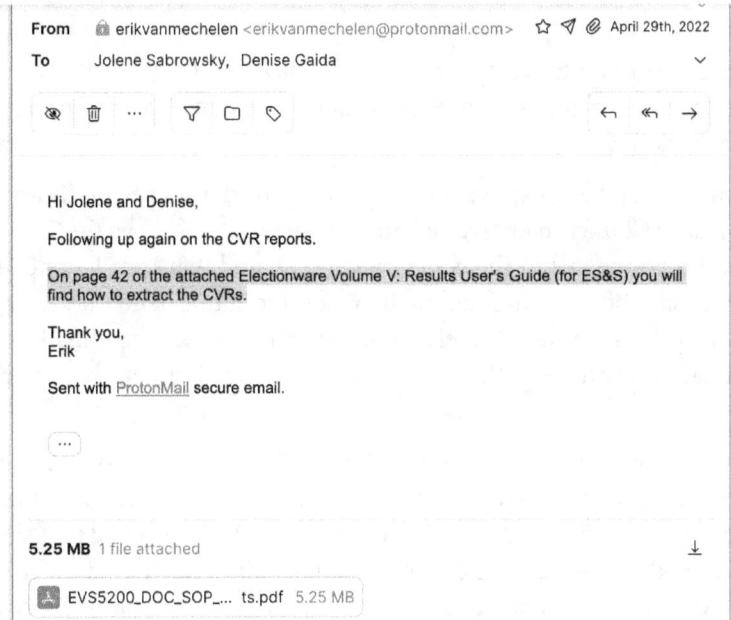

Email providing directions to extract the CVR

I have tried to sort out how CVRs might have been turned off, or if there is a language game being played, or if the CVRs might be stored somewhere else or called something else.

From a document[121] titled "Ballot Image Information on ES&S Systems issued November 1, 2018, it appears that the EVS Electionware user can specify which ballot images are to be saved on the DS200 and Central Scanners (DS450/DS850): 1) All images, 2) Write-In Images Only, 3) No images. Could these configurations at all be related to whether the CVRs are saved?

---
[121]https://edca.1dca.org/DcaDocs/2020/2445/2020-2445_Brief_1050162_RC14B202D20Supplemental2FAmended20Appendix.pdf

The technical details may not be clear, but the truth is states like Rhode Island and select counties in other states *have* received their CVRs which exposed the machine problem. Minnesota is using the same hardware and software from the same vendors as these other states.

But in Minnesota we apparently don't have CVRs, at least according to the responses Minnesotans have so far received from their county officials.

On June 24, 2022 I spoke on the phone with the county auditor in Chisago County to learn more about why they don't have the CVRs. In this phone call[122], the county auditor shared that Hart had done an onsite software upgrade about a month prior (around May 2022) which archived the 2020 election. I'm not sure whether this is in violation of the 52 USC §20701 22-month election data retention records[123].

On the phone call, the county auditor of Chisago County stated that she had already asked the vendor who said the CVRs could not be recovered. To her credit, the Chisago County Auditor stated that she had made a note to save that report in upcoming elections, to which I expressed gratitude. This is not the first time software vendors have put election officials in a bad position through software upgrades, with the most high profile example being in Mesa County, Colorado, which produced this report showing manipulation of election databases[124].

Going forward, it is also important to urge county commissioners to pass resolutions (in county commission meetings) so that election officials will turn ON cast vote record (CVR) functionality (if indeed the CVR functionality has been turned OFF) for the primary on Aug 9, 2022. If they were turned off in at least some counties in 2020, they should be turned back on.

---

[122] https://soundcloud.com/erikvanmech/chisago-hart-upgrademp3

[123] https://uscode.house.gov/view.xhtml?req=granuleid:USC-prelim-title52-section20701&num=0&edition=prelim

[124] https://magaraccoon.com/docs/MesaCountyReport3.pdf

Dominion and Hart also produced CVRs. In Hart's case, it produces a CVR (basic to counting ballots and their vote opportunities): Out of Idaho a Technical Reference Manual "Ballot Scanning and Review Software"[125] *Terms: Cast Vote Record (pages 10, 11, 14, and 189); CVR (pages 10, 11, 14, 18, 163, 164, 214) and 131, 133, 135) ...*

Pushing Back Against Tyranny

On Day 2 of the Cyber Symposium I found a chair near the front, stage left, where Dr. Frank and Mark Cook continued to explore and explain the server images provided by Tina Peters (highlighted in the [S]election Code documentary). I had noticed Captain Seth Keshel[126] come in and wanted to speak with him. Not long before this Code Monkey's lawyer had apparently suggested they not examine the server images since they may have been acquired illegally (untrue, as it is the duty of county clerks to preserve election materials and data). I learned from the person who gave me a ride from Minneapolis that a few of them in the back were looking at the same server images and feeding Dr. Frank and Mark Cook information. Dr. Frank's calming intonation, "This is *better* than PCAPs" still holds true today.

When Seth finished speaking with Wendy Rogers and Sunny Borrelli, I introduced myself. He said to focus on the collar counties around the Twin Cities like Wright, Scott, etc. Seth's point was that we would face too much opposition in counties like Hennepin, Ramsey, Dakota, or St. Louis. And given the progress teams have made in places like Wright and Dakota, his trend and political analysis was not wrong to highlight them. But as time passed it was clear that breakthroughs might also be achieved in more rural, lower population counties, of which there are many across our 87-county state.

---

[125] https://sos.idaho.gov/elect/clerk/hart/verity/Verity_Central_Technical_Reference_Manual_6600-003_A04.pdf

[126] https://captk.com

Months later, my friend Nathan and I had been thinking about where to focus in Minnesota. Nathan said, Why not Todd County? David Clements had been urging folks to find rural counties where county commissioners might be more willing to put election discussions on the agenda or even pass favorable resolutions. And, after all, Dr. Frank's refrain is "Vote Amish," a nod to elections without unneeded technology. Todd County is one of the Amish hotspots in Minnesota. So I sent Todd County a data request for their 2020 cast vote record (CVR) report on the same day I sent a request for one from Hennepin County.

I tell this story in wrapping up the chapter on the enemy's coverup to illustrate a lesson encapsulated by Stargate SG-1's Season 5, Episode 5 - Red Sky, wherein the SG-1 team causes the disruption of a sun near a planet protected by the Asgard. Unbeknownst to the locals, SG-1 seeks help from the 'Grand Council' Asgard. In the conclusion, it is unclear whether the solution attempted by the SG-1 team and the local population was successful, or if the Asgard had helped them out after all.

In other words, it's important to try. God takes care of the results in time.

And wouldn't you know it? Within moments of writing the above lines (Thursday, June 16, 2022) I stumbled upon the following page in the ES&S DS200 Operator's Manual, which resolves much of the confusion I'd had up to this point regarding cast vote records (CVR) and the seeming *lack* of any in Minnesota from the 2020 election.

Page 57 of the ES&S Operator's Manual[127] explains how if the ballot images are turned off, **so are the cast vote records**. I was so excited to find this that I immediately posted the following on my Telegram channel[128].

---

[127]https://www.dropbox.com/s/ej4d6c51knlv3u4/ES%26S%20DS%20200%20Operator%20Guide%20copy%202.pdf?dl=0

[128]https://t.me/erikmn

Erik for SOS

Scan Ballot

Use the Scan Ballot option to perform a ballot test for the DS200 and the ballot diverter if you are using a ballot diverter. The results will appear in the **Reports** menu option, located below the **Scan Ballot** menu option.

 Note: If the election is set up to save no ballot images, the DS200 will not save any ballot images or cast vote records and the public and protected counters will not increment. This is a feature specifically used for hardware testing and should not be used to validate the tabulator's mark detection accuracy during L&A.

From page 57 of the ES&S DS 200 Operator Guide:

"If the election is set up to save no ballot images, the DS200 will not save any ballot images or cast vote records..."

This may be why no Minnesotan has received any CVRs through public data requests from ANY county in Minnesota.

CVRs allow the machines to tell on themselves.

Solution:
Pass resolutions in county commissioner board meetings to have this functionality turned ON for the August 9, 2022 primary elections.

Else the machine-driven elections will lack this crucial machine audit trail.

Pg 57 of the ES&S DS200 Operator's Manual

This means that even if we *keep* the machines for the upcoming primary elections on August 9, 2022, county commissioners could pass resolutions to turn ON the cast vote records so that there is a machine trail. There is no logical push back to *not* having these ON. Our tax dollars have paid for these machines and how they count the votes should be auditable and transparent.

If cast vote records are turned ON, then candidates and the public can request the cast vote records immediatly after the primary election to verify the reported results match the machine results. If they are denied these, it should only raise further suspicion about what might be being covered up.

Even with the defense phase (cover up and destruction of evidence) of the election coup falling apart, so far no county commissions (in Minnesota) have decided to return to hand counting paper ballots as many of their constituents desire—instead, counties plan to run elections on very similar if not the same software which managed the 2020 election. This would be unwise if fair and transparent elections are desired.

I fully support the many people continuing to go to their county commissioner board meetings to inform them of available fixes to restore trust to all voters.

Then vs. Now

I want to close this chapter with a summary from Jeffrey O'Donnell posted on June 1, 2022, contrasting the August 2021 position with the June 2022 position.

The rest of this chapter are Jeff's words from this post[129]:

I joined this fight full time more than nine months ago. I wilfully pushed the pause button on our lives and trusted God to provide - and he has. I have a new appreciation for the Israelites who were given manna to survive - each day's needs are supplied. The next week or month... that's where faith and trust come in. At that time, Lindell's symposium had just happened and everyone thought the pcap information would save us. We were wrong. Specifically speaking,

---

[129] https://t.me/ALoneRaccoon/2221

- the process of defining the algorithms used to sway the election was still in its infancy, with Ed Solomon and Draza Smith only just starting to be able to describe the process
- State voter rolls were being only cursorily examined, and little comparison was being done between states
- The inner workings of the election servers was still a complete mystery
- Most analysis of the 2020 fraud was being done by people within counties. Very little information was being shared between states or even counties
- The clues to the whole thing in the Edison election night reporting were seen but not yet understood
- No effort existed to collect, analyze, and share election data such as cast vote records and ballot images. The importance of Cast Vote Records in this fight was really not recognized yet.
- Although "phantom" absentee votes were suspected, their prevalence and widespread abuse was not generally known yet.
- Protecting 2022/2024, while on people's radar, had no viable plan."

Now look at today.

- the algorithm used by the election servers is well understood and can even be predicted now
- Tremendous problems with voter rolls have been loudly documented in many states.
- We have a full understanding of the internal working of the Dominion system, with other vendors soon to come.
- There is coordination and cooperation - and healthy competition - between groups in different states
- Edison has been revealed to be a conspirator in the election plot, and while much is still not understood, the "edison zero"

and the flipping of votes between absentee and in-person has been well-documented, as has the fact that the reporting is largely theater and does not match up well with the actual results in a state/county until the very end,
- Cast Vote Records, ballot images, tabulator logs, voter rolls/histories and more have been obtained from many counties in many states, and their analysis has proved crucial. Any bit of data we get from a county is something they cannot destroy in September.
- Massive absentee ballot fraud is a fact.
- Findings from 2020 are being used in many ways to minimize the fraud potential in future elections… plus the identification of any fraud now takes minutes rather than months.
- Serious court cases (much better than the quick ones done right after the election) are progressing in numerous states"

Where are the arrests? Please do not be naïve. We are forced to be a citizen's Justice Department, because our country does not currently have a functioning one. Our burden of proof is immense and unfair. We have no subpeona or warrant power. You need to think of this for what it is - a national RICO case. Read how Guliani broke up the mobs in New York. He built his case from the ground up and quietly climbed the ladder of corruption until he had the goods on ALL the bosses. Then he struck.

Chapter Five - Minnesota in 2022

"These people don't understand."

—Isabelle, shortly after having the mic taken away from her as a delegate at the MNGOP state convention while speaking about electronic voting machines, whose mom and dad lost everything in Communist Ecuador

"Did you by chance see the second round results?"

"I, um, no, because we knew they were good. But I'm not going to worry about the results right now. Right now I'm just going to chill with my family."

—Part of a conversation between the author and Kelly Jahner-Byrne[130] soon after her concession speech

---

In the psychological realm, in mid-to-late 2020, George Floyd dominated news cycles. Covid-19 was also a daily discussion topic on and offline. This provided distraction, air cover, and justification for procedural changes which flew in the face of existing Minnesota law and took our focus off the voting machines.

Just as there were distractions in 2020, in the runup to the 2022 midterm elections, there has been no shortage of diversions attempted by those who wish to keep us from reclaiming our government.

---

[130] https://www.dropbox.com/s/yu0jtnd81avf2uf/kelly_sos_endorsement.m4a?dl=0

This Rasmussen survey shows what voters care about versus what the media cares about:

Top Voter Midterm Issues
All U.S. Likely Voters
Rasmussen Reports
June 7, 2022

1 – **Inflation** – 87% Concerned, 60% Very Concerned
2 – **Election Integrity** – 83% Concerned, 61% Very Concerned
3 – **Violent Crime** – 83% Concerned, 51% Very Concerned
4 – **Rising Gas Prices** – 82% Concerned, 60% Very Concerned
5 – **Illegal Immigration** – 77% Concerned, 50% Very Concerned
6 – **School Issues** – 76% Concerned, 58% Very Concerned

U.S. Legacy Media Top Midterm Issues
All U.S. Likely Voters
Rasmussen Reports
June 7, 2022

1 – **Abortion Rights** – 63% Concerned, 42% Very Concerned
2 – **Capitol Riot Investigation** – 59% Important, 43% Very Important
3 – **COVID-19** – 57% Concerned, 22% Very Concerned
4 – **Climate Change** – 54% Concerned, 32% Very Concerned
5 – **LGBTQ Issues** – 42% Support, 23% Strongly Support
6 – **Ukraine** – "Which do you consider more important to America's national interests?
Defending the Ukraine against Russian invasion – 36%
Defending the U.S. Southern Border against illegal immigration – 53%

61% Very Concerned About Election Integrity

Back in February, the beginning of the election process started in Minnesota at the precinct caucuses.

There, the key item of business is electing delegates. Those chosen in their precincts will then serve as delegates at the basic political organizing unit (BPOU) level. From there, another round of voting happens to elect delegates to the congressional district and state conventions, where endorsements occur for governor, attorney general, state auditor, and secretary of state.

In a world where most republican voters understood how to get involved starting in the precinct caucuses, this system has a chance to reliably produce solid candidates. That hasn't happened in the past. I too was a first timer and gradually learned how in practice the delegate selection process and ultimatly endorsements are a carefully crafted and heavily influenced outcome.

The Party says it wants to support endorsed candidates and discourages coverage of non-endorsed candidates. Meanwhile, the MNGOP has shown in reality it doesn't fully respect its own endorsements. For example, Mark Bishofksy[131], endorsed candidate for 33B who single-handedly kickstarted the Stop the Mandate[132] movement and hosted medical freedom rallies with thousands at the Capitol, is facing a challenger arguably more liked by the MNGOP leadership. Why is the MNGOP supporting this candidate in a race against the already endorsed candidate where elsewhere Party representatives pressure event organizers not to speak with non-endorsed candidates?

What I've observed is that the MNGOP, a private entity, works very hard to control who eventually becomes an endorsed candidate, even pulling stunts to avoid the endorsement of candidates like Nathan Wesenberg in SD10 that are a threat to their current grip on power. It's only a matter of time before the majority of people see what they've been up to and reclaim what has been taken from them.

This chapter does not go easy on anyone but also cannot begin to

---

[131] https://markformnhouse.com/
[132] https://stopthemandatemn.org/

document the full extent of transgressions the Party has made upon its own constitution, rules, members, and regular republican voters. The point of sharing just a few examples is to allow the people experiencing this pressure from the Party to know they are not alone in their treatment, and also to encourage others to come forward and speak about what they've seen.

The Preparation Phase in Minnesota for 2022

The preparation phase as described by Patrick Colbeck is in full swing around the country and in Minnesota.

It boils down to:

1. maneuvering desired candidates onto the ballot and using influence operations to promote them
2. keeping in place election laws and rules which tend to weaken election fairness and transparency
3. most important – keeping the machines

It matters a lot which candidates are on the ballot for a primary or general election. Imagine if Jeb Bush or Ted Cruz had faced off against Hillary Clinton in 2016, instead of Donald Trump. In that dystopia, some percentage of republican voters may have stayed home and Hillary may have won easily. Unexciting candidates lead to low legitimate turnout. But if voters stay home a vote can be cast in their stead through real-time monitoring in the manner already described in the Attack Phase.

The method of putting forward unexciting candidates is also effective in state and local elections. As the media and the Republican establishment tries to get us talking about a red wave, we must stay vigilant and put forward America First candidates. A red wave of establishment candidates could spell the end of our country.

To avoid that disaster requires that America First candidates stand up and join races, from school board to county commissioner to senate. It does no one any good to elect candidates who can be influenced away from the principles of upholding the constitution when the enemy is no longer at the gates but is fully occupying our territory.

Election laws in Minnesota continue to allow drop boxes, even though some areas have passed resolutions to remove them. Absentee voting and early voting are still legal for everyone, not only for distant military or the legitimately sick.

Electronic voting machines, from epollbooks to tabulators to election management systems, are still very much in play and it's conceivable that the cast vote records (CVR) reports will again *not* be turned ON, leaving Minnesotans without a trustworthy machine audit trail. If machines count the votes and they aren't fully auditable, election results can't be trusted.

MNGOP Pressures Republicans

In Clay County, attempts were made by party operatives to remove the BPOU chair Edwin Hahn[133]—in a locked room in the library led by Michelle Fischbach staffer Calvin Benson. The Chair of the Clay County BPOU sent this cease and desist letter[134] to David Haan on March 30, 2022.

---

[133] https://youtu.be/dMfCeMuLuZc?t=522
[134] https://drive.google.com/file/d/1s4ANas8A8tOai0Qiw-dXMpzCKjHcv4km/view

REPUBLICANS OF CLAY COUNTY
Basic Political Operating Unit (BPOU)
P.O. BOX 943 MOORHEAD, MN 56561

OFFICE OF
EDWIN HAHN
CHAIR

(218) 686-3970
chair@republicansofclaycounty.com

March 30, 2022

David Hann
7400 Metro Boulevard
Edina, MN 55439

Re: Notice to IMMEDIATELY cease and desist interfering in the local management of the Clay County Republican BPOU

Dear Chair Hann:

This letter is to serve as formal notice that you must immediately cease and desist interfering in the management of the Clay County BPOU that is outside the scope of the state party functions, and stop putting out false information about the fraudulent proceeding that took place in Clay County on March 8, 2022.

Additionally, this letter serves as formal notice that you and the MNGOP staff and volunteers must immediately cease and desist in making slanderous and false public statements about me directly to people, through press releases or posts on social media.

The following information supports this demand:

The attempted efforts to first remove me as Clay County BPOU Chair and then cancel the scheduled BPOU Convention, was orchestrated by a small number of disgruntled members of the BPOU, and violated the Constitution of the Clay County Republicans and Robert's Rules of Order.

This group of four or five people refused to join the official meeting, which was called to order AFTER these individuals refused multiple requests from multiple people to join the entire Executive Committee meeting AND were informed by a long-time Clay County BPOU parliamentarian that their meeting would be out of order. **It was then reported, by MN Senator, and candidate for Governor, Michelle Benson's son, Calvin, that the group had permission from the state party to hold the meeting.**

Cease and Desist Letter sent to MNGOP Chair David Haan

The Party has not quit its antics to hold onto power while more and more regular people are dismayed by the lengths they will go to do so.

In Polk County, the BPOU Chair was recently sent this letter[135] by the Party after he set up a training course[136] to be held on July 16. In doing so, the Party claims Jon Ross and others are "involved in efforts to organize against endorsed Republican candidates."

REPUBLICAN PARTY OF MINNESOTA
7400 Metro Boulevard, Edina, MN 55439

To:
Bill Oliver, Chair of Marshall County Republicans
Chris Morinville, Chair of Red Lake County Republicans
Patrick McCoy, Chair of Pennington County Republicans
Jon Ross, Chair of Polk County Republicans
Heather Kirby, Chair of Norman County Republicans

Notice of violation: CEASE AND DESIST - Final Warning

It has come to our attention that you and other officers of your BPOUs have been involved in various efforts to organize against endorsed Republican candidates. These efforts include but are not limited to: meetings and trainings; involve the use of Republican Party property; the Republican Party name and logo; the use of proprietary Party lists including state and CD7 delegates and alternates outside of your respective BPOUs; and more.

We have received evidence of your promotion of these efforts via email to individuals using official Republican party name, logo, and lists. These are property of the Republican Party of Minnesota, the Republican National Committee, and the Congressional District 7 Republican Party of Minnesota respectively.

MNGOP scrambles to hold onto power

These aren't the only tactics Party operatives have used.

In Kittson County, Amanda and Dave Hughes came under attack after Dave Hughes[137] decided to challenge for the Minnesota State Senate in District 1 versus the establishment's Mark Johnson.

According to Amanda, the Executive Director of the Campaign Finance Board (CFB) was contacted in early June by Ron Huettl, Finance Director of the Republican Party of Minnesota, with a "serious concern" over the fact that the Kittson Rebuplicans are not filing with the CFB. Ron never called Amanda or Dave. So what were Ron's intentions?

---

[135] https://www.dropbox.com/s/lb2k888hp69k5s8/1655998272163_06-15-2022%20SD%201%20Cease%20and%20Desist%20Letter%20FINAL.pdf?dl=0

[136] https://facl-training.org/schools/events/east-grand-forks-mn-pls-16jul2022

[137] https://ballotpedia.org/Dave_Hughes

Republican Party of Minnesota

7400 Metro Blvd, Suite 424, Edina, MN 55439
Office: 651-222-0022   Fax: 651-224-4122

Amanda Hughes
P.O. 248
Karlstad, MN 56732

Dear Amanda:

We have recently been informed by the Minnesota Campaign Finance Board (CFB) that the Kittson County Republican organization, for which you have served as Chair, has not been registered as a sub-unit (BPOU) of the Minnesota Republican Party since 2010. They have also informed us that the Kittson County Republican organization will be investigated by the CFB to determine if any campaign finance laws have been violated back to 2010. If violations are found, the CFB will assess penalties.

Given the fact that you have failed to comply with campaign finance law and have lost your status as a BPOU of the Minnesota Republican Party, we are requiring you to send to the MNGOP all funds currently in your bank account as well as all the bank statements received during your tenure as Chair. Furthermore, no one in your Kittson County organization may lawfully continue to use the name or logo of the Kittson County Republican Party or claim to represent the Republican Party in any official capacity. Any use of Party data including Data Center, Delegate and Alternate lists and any other Party information by the Kittson County organization is also prohibited.

We are disappointed that the Kittson County organization has failed to fulfill its duty as a BPOU of the Minnesota Republican Party. The Congressional District 7 Republican organization, at their discretion, will determine when and if a Kittson County BPOU will be re-constituted.

Sincerely,

David Hann
Chair
MNGOP

Lee Prinkkila
Treasurer
MNGOP

cc: Craig Bishop, Chair – CD7

Chair Haan's weak and illegitimate attempt to dissolve the Kittson BPOU

On June 23, 2022, the Kittson Republicans Treasurer Jacob Bakke received this confirmation from the Executive Director of the CFB, showing there were no issues from the perspective of the CFB. The Executive Director confirms the Kittson Republicans need not register if they have incomes less than $750 per year. And there is no investigation.

June 23, 2022

Jacob Bakke Sent via email: jmbakke1@gmail.com
Treasurer, Kittson County Republicans

Dear Mr. Bakke:

I received your email concerning the Kittson County Republican party unit (BPOU) of the Minnesota Republican Party. From your email, and the phone conversation I had with Mr. Hughes, I understand that the Kittson County Republicans did not raise, contribute, or spend over $750 in a calendar year during the period of 2011 to 2021, and has not reached the $750 threshold so far in 2022. The requirement to register as a party unit with the Campaign Finance Board is triggered by exceeding the $750 threshold for financial activity during a calendar year. Until the Kittson County Republican party unit exceeds the $750 threshold there is no registration, reporting, or other filing requirement with the Board.

I can confirm that the Kittson County Republican party unit was registered with the Board, but that the party unit terminated its registration with the Board on October 19, 2010. At that time the party unit had a cash balance of less than $100. There were no reports or other documents outstanding when the Kittson County Republican party unit terminated the registration.

I can confirm that the Board has not authorized an investigation or audit of the Kittson County Republican party unit. Staff conducts formal investigations and audits at the direction of the Board; or in response to a complaint filed with the Board that alleges a violation of the Minnesota Statutes the Board administers. In either case the individual or association that may be investigated or audited is notified and given the opportunity to appear before the Board to explain why an investigation or audit is not needed.

I hope I have responded to the points you raised in your email, please feel free to contact me if you need additional information.

Regards,

Jeff Sigurdson
Executive Director
(651)539-1189

Suite 190 • Centennial Office Building • 658 Cedar Street • St. Paul, MN 55155-1603
651-539-1180 • 800-657-3889 • Fax 651-539-1196 • 800-357-4114 • cf.board@state.mn.us
For TTY/TDD communication, contact us through the Minnesota Relay Service at 800-627-3529

Confirmation from the CFB that there is no investigation and all is well

Chair Hann doesn't have the authority to dissolve a BPOU. Only the Kittson Republicans can.

The Kittson Republicans exist because they organized, wrote and passed a Constitution and elected officers. Their status isn't based on our registration with the CFB.

The group is small. There were only about 1,500 republican voters in the 2020 general election.

Amanda said: "Destroying party structure shouldn't be the agenda of the Chair." I agree 100% with her.

"Of course it's not about that," said Amanda. "We have two Republicans running in SD1. No other candidates. The Primary winner sails through the general without spending a penny. So this is because my husband is challenging Mark Johnson."

Forgive them for they know not what they do; the context—their diminishing power—demands these actions of them. They think they will get away with this. But now *you* know the truth, so they have not.

If you are part of or connected to the Republican Party, it is important to hold your own leadership to account. Ask them why they are trying to disrupt Clay County, Kittson County, and Polk County. These are not the only places stories have emerged, loud and clear. This call to action includes BPOU chairs and your average conservative, republican voter. (This book will be emailed to every BPOU chair in Minnesota.)

Confirmed and Documented Tampering of Delegate Lists

Right from the jump, there were issues at the precinct caucuses. Numerous reports of tampering[138] in [Otter Tail County], Morrison

---
[138] https://saveminnesota.org/evidence

County, and Clay County (but not only there) suggested delegate lists were being changed either at the BPOU level or the state level (or both). Unless an audit was done, reconciling the eyewitness and documented accounts would be difficult. No audits were done.

Seeing how the confirmed reports of delegate tampering[139] were (or weren't) handled, I couldn't help wondering how many more delegate list incidents went unnoticed and therefore unreported. I emailed my BPOU Chair about this to see whether our lists could be confirmed.

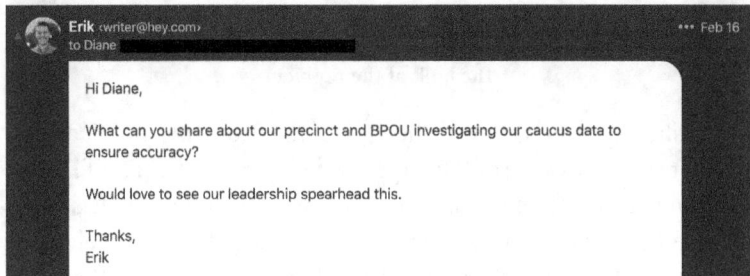

Feb 16 email to my BPOU Chair

Diane responded suggesting this happened because of previous delegates somehow including previous delegate attendees.

---

[139]https://www.action4liberty.com/corruption_in_morrison_county_gop

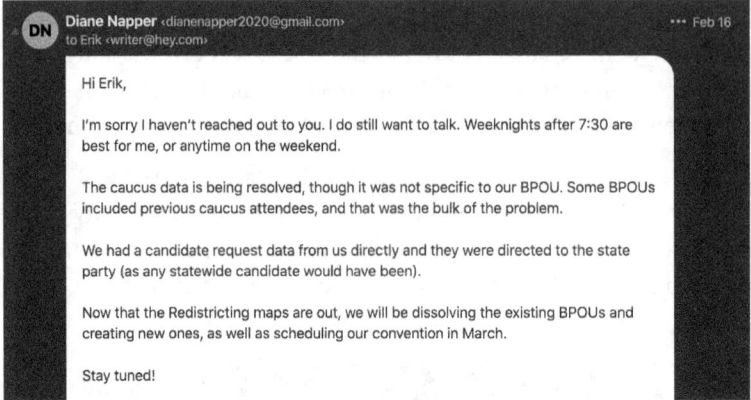

The bulk of the problem

When she suggests "that was the bulk of the problem" it indicates to me that she was aware of the larger issue (or various kinds of issues) bubbling up in other areas. And why would other BPOUs have included previous caucus attendees on their lists? Only delegates elected at the precinct caucuses become delegates or alternates. Having previously been on a delegate list does not qualify someone to be a delegate in the future.

I responded the next day.

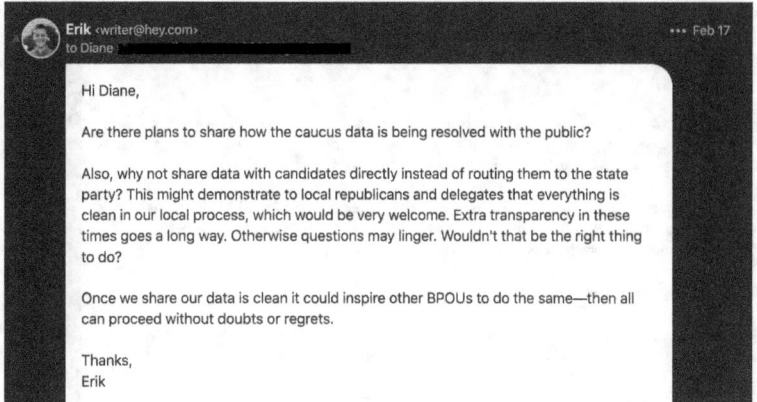

A request for more transparency

Her response doesn't answer all of my questions and suggests she was taking direction from the state party.

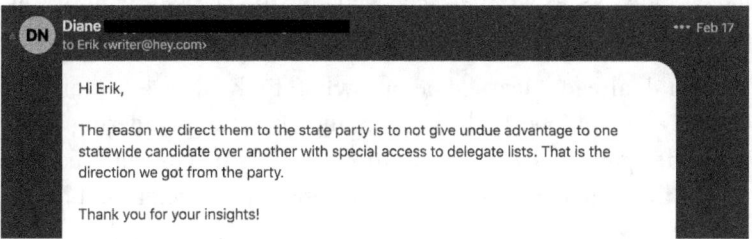

Feb 17 reply from my BPOU Chair

I sent one more email which did not recieve a reply.

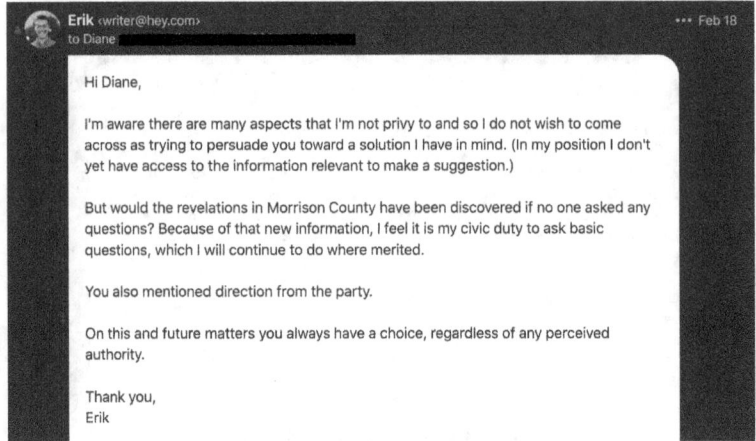

Feb 18 to BPOU Chair

I am thankful that Diane engaged in this email thread, because I haven't always, as we shall see, been able to get email replies from everyone in MNGOP, in particular the leadership.

What I'd already learned about what took place in Morrison County[140] combined with this exchange had me wondering: How many delegates at BPOU conventions, endorsing conventions, and finally the state convention would ultimately be illegitimate?

For just one example that soon emerged, consider the delegate lists from Otter Tail County[141].

---

[140] https://soundcloud.com/user-191695017/caucus-conventions-and-corruption-in-the-mngop-with-nathan-wesenberg-part-1-of-2

[141] https://saveminnesota.org/otter-tail/f/otter-tail-report-election-tampering-in-10-precincts

	Challenged Precincts	Caucus Election			MNGOP List	
		Delegates	Alternates		Delegates	Alternates
1	Candor Twp	1	0		4	3
2	Erhard City	0	0		1	0
3	Fergus Falls W-1 P-2	6	0		6	3
4	Fergus Falls W-2 P-2	7	8		7	10
5	Fergus Falls W-2 P-3	1	1		1	2
6	New York Mills City	4	0		5	0
7	Parkers Prairie City	4	0		5	2
8	Perham City	10	1		11	1
9	Pine Lake Twp	0	0		2	0
10	Vergas City	0	0		2	4
	TOTALS	33	10		44	25
	DISCREPANCY				11	15

Otter Tail Delegate List Discrepancies

From this detailed report[142] it was discovered that "two individuals whose eligibility is in question, were elected at the March 19th County Convention to represent the county at the State and Congressional District Conventions – one as a delegate, the other as an alternate." The opening sentence of the conclusion of this report reads: "If caucus precinct delegations have been systemically altered, it would appear to undermine the foundational integrity of our democratic process."

Having reviewed some of these reports[143] and having spoken with dozens of people about delegate lists from across the state, including people like Nathan Wesenberg in this conversation[144], my gut feeling says that perhaps as much as 12-15% of state convention delegates in Rochester may not have been legitimate. Remember, this could be more *or* less, but since BPOUs and the Party were not able to demonstrate reconciliation of the lists, we may never know.

The lack of a tight yet transparent chain of custody of the data

---

[142] https://drive.google.com/file/d/1Mq8vRXwOQTw9ZsQQCm3MRIYwrD_khx10/view
[143] https://saveminnesota.org/evidence
[144] https://soundcloud.com/user-191695017/caucus-conventions-and-corruption-in-the-mngop-with-nathan-wesenberg-part-1-of-2

is as much an issue with these lists as it is with our votes cast at conventions or in primary or general elections.

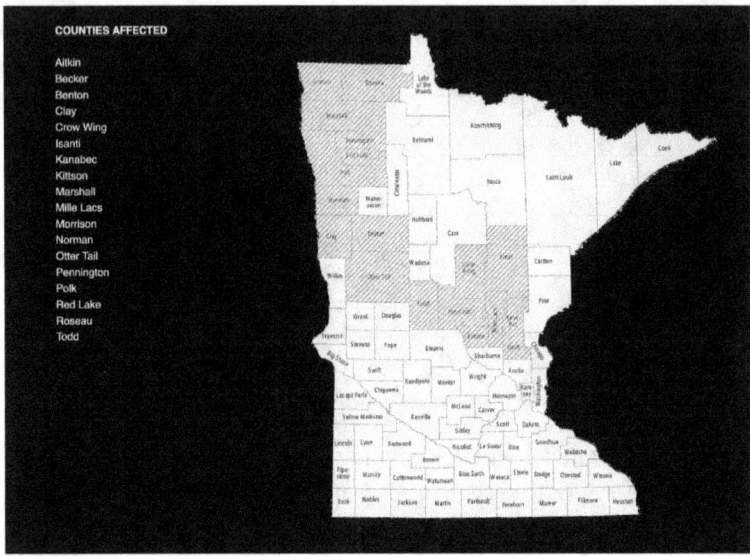

Counties Affected So Far - saveminnesota.org

Even if we conservatively speculated that only about 1 state delegate per county (87 counties) should not have been included (replacing someone else), then that would represent a large voting bloc shift. If only about 100 people were replaced, that is a potential swing of a net 200 votes, about a 10% swing as there were about 2,200 seated casting votes for the endorsing segments in Rochester. Of course, no one is duty bound to vote for one candidate or another in advance, but if it is true that delegates were being replaced—and that has been shown to be the case—why was that being done?

From one point of view, the result is equivalent to inflating voter rolls (in the statewide voter registration system). From another vantage point, the result is equivalent to a vote swap in an election management system[145].

---

[145] https://rumble.com/vgi89t-hacking-democracy-antrim-county-mi-edition.html

Note: Even though I am a candidate for secretary of state, I never received delegate lists from the MNGOP as other candidates were provided—in case as a delegate you were wondering why you may not get emails from me. Therefore I am reaching the people of Minnesota through this book.

Endorsing Conventions

Endorsing conventions allow the MNGOP to select an "endorsed" candidate, who will get to carry that badge forward. These conventions happen at the senate district, congressional district, and state level.

How do you get to participate and vote in these conventions?

By becoming a delegate.

Starting at the precinct level, then the BPOU level (Basic Political Organizing Unit), then the congressional district and finally the state convention.

At each stage you may nominate yourself and then your peers must elect you to move forward.

Eventually, a bit over 2,000 delegates make their way to the state convention to select the endorsed candidates for state auditor, secretary of state, attorney general, and governor. These 2,000 delegates have tremendous influence because they are determining the endorsed candidate on behalf of about 1.5 million republican voters in Minnesota.

Candidates without the endorsement can still run as republicans in the primary elections, this year happening on August 9. The winners of the democratic and republican primaries face off in the midterm elections on November 8, 2022.

Precinct caucus took place on February 1, 2022. There were five people total at my table, including my neighbor, his wife, and his son, plus one more woman thankfully wearing the only mask in the room. Because our precinct was alotted five BPOU delegate slots, each of us was able to nominate ourselves and become delegates without any speeches or voting. A couple of us had brought resolutions we wanted sent up to the next stage for consideration. One close to my heart was a resolution to remove electronic voting equipment. (Please note, this is quite different from a resolution drafted by a county commission to remove electronic voting equipment, which if passed in a county commissioner board meeting has real weight.)

Of note was (I believe) an unnecessary governor straw poll, which we were urged to complete by a certain time. One benefit of the straw poll was the opportunity to learn that while about 10,000 republicans voted in it in 2018, more than 17,000 did so in 2022.

Also of note was the attendance of friends who had voted for democrats in the previous election but had come looking for something new. I hope they read or listen to this book so they can see I might have observed some of the things they also did.

At the BPOU stage in my district, about 34 of the delegates elected at the precinct caucus showed up. There were only 9 slots for delegates moving onto the congressional district convention and the state convention.

I almost *didn't* become a delegate.

Having missed the pre-signup (by email?), I only got onto the list to be considered with a few minutes to spare by leaving my seat, going across the room, and asking my BPOU Chair Diane to be included. There was a printed list to which I added my handwritten name. Several others, also apparently unaware of how to get their names on that printed list (printed prior to the meeting), saw me walk over and also did so to get their names written down for consideration. The printed list was 12 people and jumped to about 19. Since we were vying for one of 9 slots, each of us then gave 30-second speeches as to why we should become delegates.

I said I care about election integrity and plan to support candidates demonstrating courage and a dedication to the truth.

Carleton Crawford, former acting chair and former deputy chair for the MNGOP and current employee of Hennepin County, gave an interesting speech. He said he was going to list himself as an alternate, so no need to vote for him. But please consider voting for those who have put in the time and effort previously into the Party.

Why did I find that interesting? His words could be seen as an encouraging nod to his workmates but also as a clever influence tactic to ensure the regulars got enough votes to move into the next round. Would anyone have cried foul if my speech suggested we needed to have 9 new delegates this year?

I asked to observe the vote counting.

Notably, I was almost shortchanged one vote but pointed it out—it was quickly amended. My simplye speech garnered me the fourth-most votes after the Chair, her husband (a senate candidate), and the BPOU secretary.

Near the basement entrance to VFW Post 494 in Crystal, MN, I was soon asked whether I would like to wear a sticker by a man working with one of the campaigns. When I declined he said, "I understand not wanting to be a walking poster." Nodding, I pulled back my jacket to reveal my t-shirt and said, "But I already am."

The t-shirt read:

Minnesota, No. 1 in Voter ~~Turnout~~ Fraud

Instead of a walking poster for any one candidate, I would go on to advocate for the issue I was surprised to learn that few wanted to discuss that day.

At this, the CD5 Convention of the Minnesota Republican Party, nearly 17 months after the November 3rd, 2020 General Election, very few if any speakers acknowledged that the election was rigged and none mentioned electronic voting equipment (epollbooks, tabulators, election management systems). Stating the obvious would surely have scored them political points (or so I thought) so why was almost everyone shying away? Only by plainly stating the problem is there any chance of going about fixing it. What's more, at that late hour, we were already at a moment where surface level issues of the election coup were obvious—because elections have consequences we are witnessing the decades long result of leaders being (s)elected, not elected.

It is easy to complain and feel good about knowing some fact that your neighbor may not yet know. But now the focus should be on solutions and taking action toward them. In the realm of elections, there are simple remedies to the overly complex and easily exploitable system currently in place.

A few hours after returning from the CD5 convention, I woke up around 2am. Restless, I soon took to writing my observations from the previous evening, what I've come to refer to as "the CD5 show"[146].

Besides the lack of substantive noises about election integrity, the big event was Cicely Davis and Royce White and Shukri Abdirahman competing for the CD5 endorsement.

There was a miscount in the first round of voting. The miscount would have given Cicely Davis the 60% threshold in the first round. But that was inaccurate, and she didn't quite make it.

Then Shukri gave a short speech saying she was dropping out to

---

[146] https://erikvanmechelen.substack.com/p/the-cd5-show

help Cicely. One person in my BPOU had left (he was unsure about Cicely and may have voted for Royce) and others may have too. This time, in round 2, 75% voted for Cicely, including myself.

I immediately sensed it was the wrong decision which did not put me in a good mood.

Was it true as was reported that Royce had offended some of the delegates? Perhaps. But what he said, I think, would have rung true with the general republican voting population (numbering about 1.5 million and probably more by now), as well as independents and democrats who are tired of the deteriorating state and country currently under occupation.

The Secretary of State Endorsement

I announced my decision to run for secretary of state[147] on May 3, 2022, standing on the back of a pickup truck in the Sherburne County Government Center parking lot, ahead of a County Commissioners Board meeting where Sherburne county residents were making the case to the commissioners to put election integrity on the agenda (short of an agenda item, there is a limited number of speakers and time, three minutes per speaker, in open forum).

Then I emailed several of the MNGOP leadership. Realizing that the convention would start nine days later, I wanted to do everything I could to be included and reduce any extra effort I would cause having entered later than Kim and Kelly.

---

[147] https://rumble.com/v13i4tm-mn-secretary-of-state-announcement.html

[2] New SOS candidate for endorsement

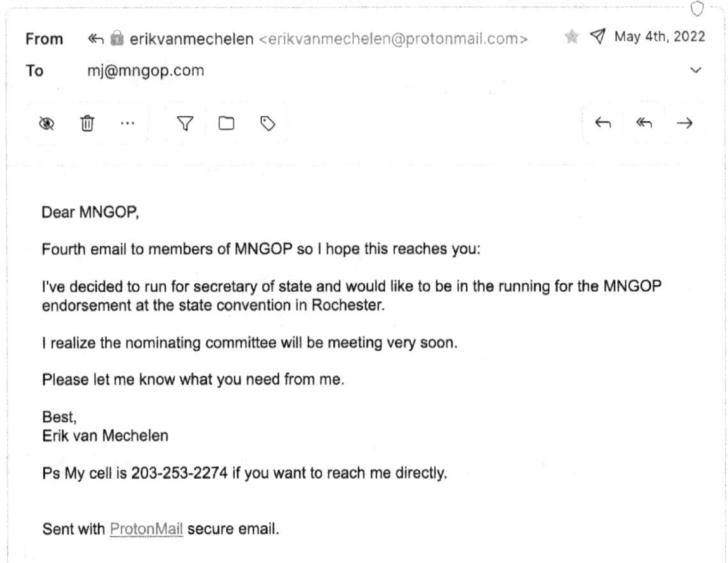

Trying to reach the MNGOP leadership

When I still didn't hear back, I contacted my BPOU Chair Diane.

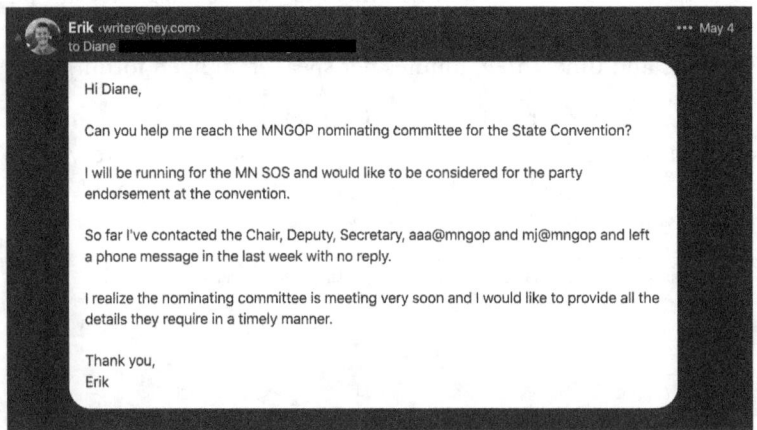

May 4 email to Diane, asking my BPOU Chair for help

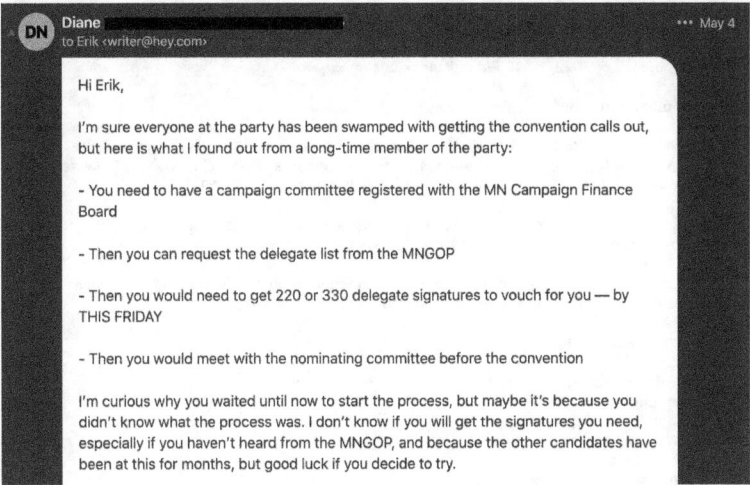

May 4 reply from Diane

On May 4th, I got a call back from Donna Bergstrom. I said I was thankful for her help and she said, "That's what we're here for."

When I wasn't copied on emails Donna said she would send to get the process rolling, I called her back the next day. We did not have another phone call but she did say to email Executive Director of the MNGOP, Mike Longergan at mj@mngop.com (which readers will note I already did above).

[4] SOS Candidate for State Convention

On Thu, May 5, 2022, 10:47 PM erikvanmechelen <erikvanmechelen@protonmail.com> wrote:
Good evening, Mike,

I had a good phone call Tuesday with Donna and she has sent me your way to ensure I've completed steps the nominations committee requires to be included in endorsement process for the state convention for secretary of state.

Realize all are diligently gearing up for next weekend so I am thankful for your help and looking forward to seeing everyone in Rochester very soon.

From others with insight into previous requirements for nominations committee I went ahead and gathered a few items but would like your guidance on the details.

At the moment I have:

-CFB registration submitted
-Announcement made
-Signature collection under way
-Lit pieces and posters printed

What other to-dos are necessary?

I'll complete them right away to follow the MNGOP guidelines.

Thank you,
Erik

Ps Donna also mentioned the delegate list link was missing from the action center of the MNGOP site. She also said she'd put me in touch with someone to potentially organize/rent a room at the convention. For me these items are lower priority than actually being considered for endorsement.

203-253-2274 is my phone to reach me directly.

2nd Email to Mike, this time after Donna Bergstrom phone call

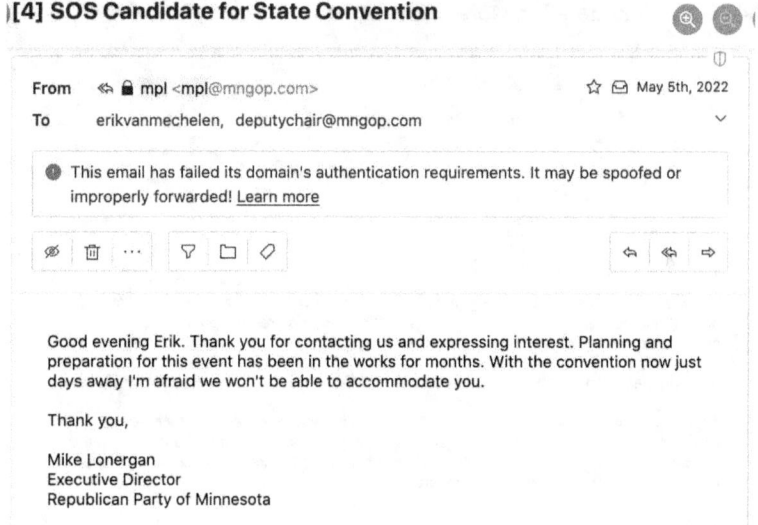

Reply from Mike same day

Chapter Five - Minnesota in 2022

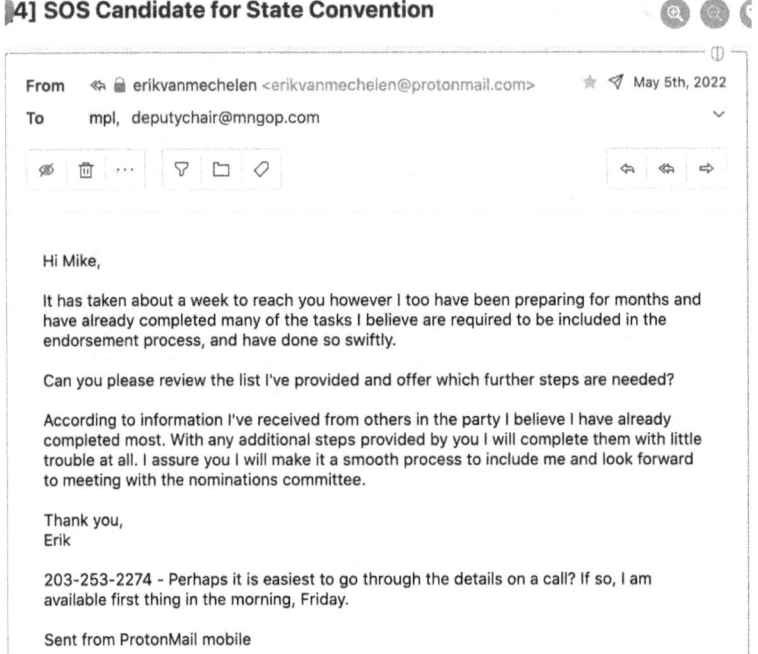

Reply to Mike's email the same evening

[2] New SOS candidate for endorsement

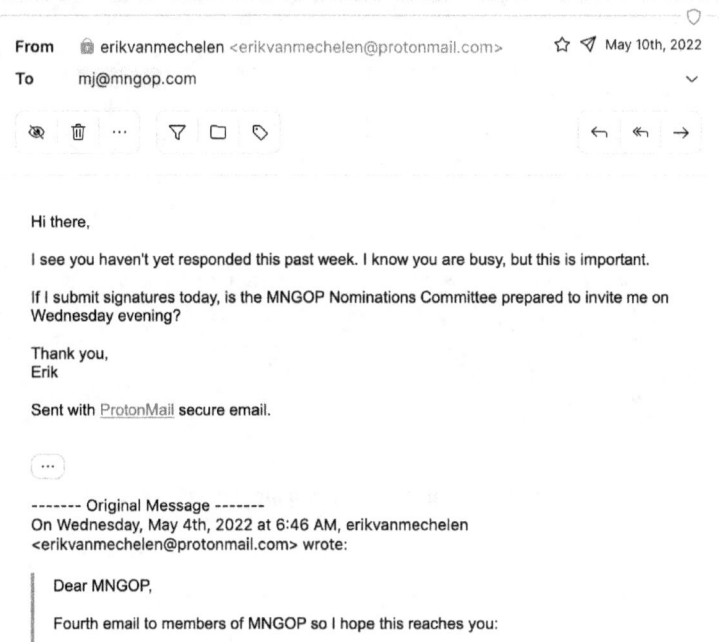

After no phone call, trying to be included

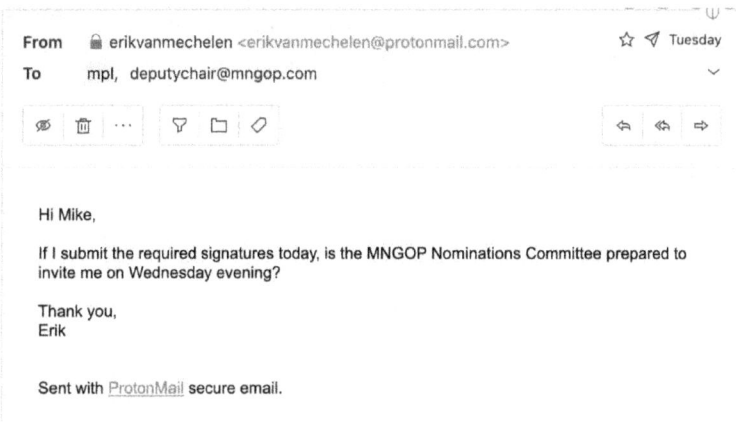

Another request to be included in Nominations Committee

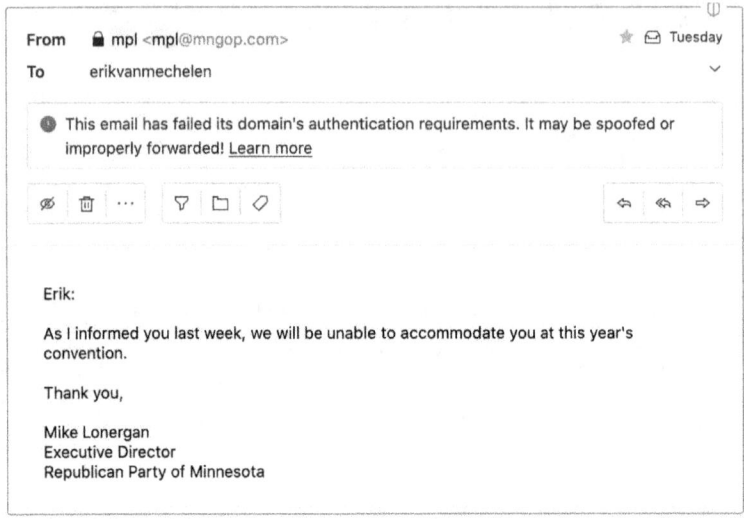

We will be unable to accommodate you

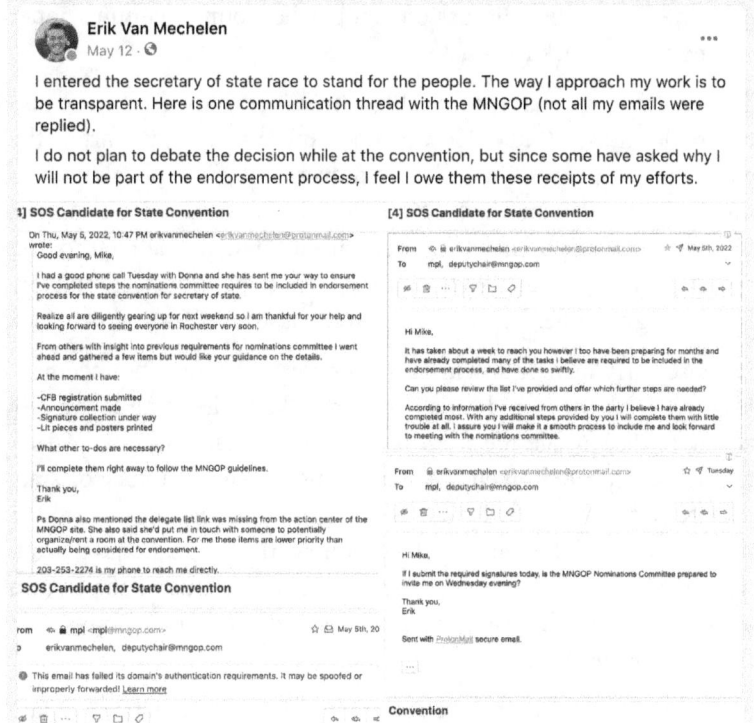

Facebook post on May 12 to supporters

Of note is the fact that Mike said already on May 5th that I would not be accommodated prior to the proposed rule deadline the following morning on May 6th. Of course, since he did not state this as the reason for non-accommodation, it remains unknown the reason why this decision was made, and by whom. At the end of the day, the MNGOP is a private entity and is legally able to make decisions like these even if they may violate their own MNGOP constitution or convention rules.

I may not have published these emails in this book if not for the growing trend of MNGOP members trying to stop discussion on election integrity like this presentation in Rochester on election machines[148] or this discussion about the county commissioner strategy with Mark Bishofsky[149].

This continuing behavior from Party members only gives me cause to wonder if the MNGOP leadership didn't want me as part of the endorsement process in order to prevent me from speaking and introducing myself to the 2,000+ delegates in Rochester. One might further wonder whether they were afraid of someone mentioning the Crime of the Century which they seem to have been completely fine with given their near silence on the issue.

In those early days following the secretary of state announcement I received messages and calls from several people, some seemingly trying to discourage me from the decision I'd already made. That was to be expected given the significance of the secretary of state role. Note for instance the congruity of actions amongst a number of secretaries of state around the country; they repeat ad nauseam how secure the election in their state was while refusing to perform actual audits and demeaning anyone asking honest questions about the process, machines, or results.

My own BPOU Chair asked why I'd chosen secretary of state instead of house rep. She thought I would face stiff competition but wished me luck. On May 31st, the final day of the filing deadline, and 12 days after I'd officially filed for secretary of state on May 18th, someone from the Party called to ask whether I'd like to run for house instead.

After sharing with a few people an early version of my website which included a segment of this book, it was forwarded (with my permission) to a woman named Donna who said she was volunteering with Kim's campaign. I accepted a phone call. Would I like to meet Kim?, she asked. The suggestion, not confirmed with Kim, was maybe I could be Kim's campaign manager since she was apparently on the lookout for one. Sure, I'll talk with Kim,

---

[148]https://rumble.com/v18c88v-machines-in-minnesota-june-12-2022.html
[149]https://rumble.com/v18p9ol-30-minutes-with-mark-bishofsky-about-election-improvements-in-minnesota.html

but can we do it soon? I asked this because I had not yet made my announcement nor informed the MNGOP. A few days passed and there was no meeting or word back, so as I was going to be at the Sherburne rally before the county commmissioners meeting on Tuesday May 3, I decided to make the announcement[150].

The woman who had called me was apparently not happy when she heard the news, but I felt I'd done the best I could to make myself available to Kim's team, if that's what they actually wanted, without further delaying my announcement. Did delaying my announcement give the MNGOP easier reason to not accommodate me? Or would they have declined anyway? We may never know.

Then, a few days prior to the convention, I took a more than one hour phone call with a man named Chris who said he wasn't working for Kim but who seemed to be helping her campaign. It was hard to gauge the purpose of the call except that Chris was curious to learn more of my thoughts on elections and to know whether I would run. He several times said he enjoyed reading the information on the website. Overall a good conversation with just one red flag going up when he said he didn't think Rick Weible's information was very compelling for non-technical people. Having at that point seen and done video recordings of Rick's work, I had a different opinion. Without Rick's educational presentations and supporting of multiple people and groups across more than a dozen Minnesota counties (and South Dakota), it's hard to say where the grassroots election integrity movements would be right now.

I spoke with Chris at the convention, too, who was able to pull over Kim as well as her husband Marty on Day 2. At the time Kim seemed to be preoccupied with the signage issues (some signs lacked the "paid for by..." language) and indicated it may be better to meet in the coming week. Marty, meanwhile, didn't seem convinced there was machine fraud in Minnesota after apparently speaking on these issues often in prior years. That was too bad

---

[150]https://rumble.com/v13i4tm-mn-secretary-of-state-announcement.html

because we were all there and could easily have discussed whatever Chris hoped we could discuss.

Post convention, Rick Weible said Marty called him asking whether Rick could get me to *not* run for secretary of state. Was this part of the purpose of the huddle at the convention?

Also, prior to the convention, there was some unfounded speculation that it was Rick's decision for me to run.

Let me clear that up.

It was my decision.

I follow no one but Jesus.

If I take guidance from anyone it's the Boss[151].

The day before the huddle with Kim, Marty, and Chris, on Friday May 12, I watched the secretary of state speeches from the alternates balcony. I'd gone up to meet a friend of a friend. I felt bad for the alternates who had to sit up here and not be included, but it was a useful vantage point to take in the spectacle. That's what the state convention could be reduced to, in a word. Others called it a circus. A useful metaphor. But the use of spectacle as a *tactic* was also plentifully demonstrated.

---

[151] https://www.dropbox.com/s/j0ie2tfrnvvdvf7/the_boss.MP4?dl=0

A spectacle to influence endorsement outcomes

Flashing lights, music, speakers on stage with huge video screens behind them. Posters covering every square inch of the walls. T-shirts, "literature", flags. A lot of emotional but often boring speeches lacking content. Talk of a red wave with a conspicuous lack of attention—not so much as a mention from the establishment speakers—of the Crime of the Century. Having seen email replies from elected officials and members of the Party during the summer of 2021—many of which if published would make them look very weak—I perhaps could have expected them to be silent, but with the increasing queasiness throughout conservative ranks that something deeper was wrong than just losing an election to run-of-the-mill democrats, I thought maybe more would speak up. At least Neil Shah said he thought his vote counted in 2016 but wasn't so sure it did in 2020.

In their secretary of state candidate speeches, neither Kim[152] nor

---

[152] https://www.youtube.com/watch?v=YfdnlYLCZ70

Kelly[153] used the words stolen election or election fraud. There was one mention of ensuring computers not be connected to the internet (in Kim's speech), but that was the only verbal mention of machines. No other comments on electronic voting equipment nor focus put onto the larger and increasingly centralized modern electronic voting system, nor a description of how its lack of certification under the VVSG 2.0 guidelines may violate Minnesota's election code.

That was a bit depressing but it emphasized to me that there was work right in front of me to do, which I was thankful for.

Kim didn't get the endorsement in the first round, ending up a few percentage points shy of the required 60%. We went onto round 2: the delegates voted again. I voted no endorsement twice (I wasn't the only one to do so) because I couldn't vote for a candidate that hadn't acknowledged the stolen election nor emphasized the necessity to minimize voter fraud going forward, including by supporting the removal of the uncertified cheat machines.

After the roughly ten minute delay from the votes going through the Padgett electronic devices into the software tallying computers (to be reviewed by the Party) and finally up onto the big screen, I was surprised *not* to see the results be displayed; instead, Kelly came out, thanked her volunteers, and conceded. Since I voted, and so did over 2,000 delegates, I wanted to know the result of the election. That seemed like the right thing to do, too.

God helped me catch up with both Kelly and Kim right after Kelly's concession speech.

The conversation with Kelly[154] left me with questions.

From the conversation:

ERIK: "Did you by chance see the second round results?"

---

[153]https://youtu.be/EMyO6Vfld8k
[154]https://www.dropbox.com/s/yu0jtnd81avf2uf/kelly_sos_endorsement.m4a?dl=0

KELLY: "I, um, no, because we knew they were good. But I'm not going to worry about the results right now. Right now I'm just going to chill with my family."

I don't know who the "we" is that Kelly is refering to. I assume "they" refers to the results. But wasn't Kelly eager to verify that her opponent actually won? And if she wasn't shown the vote totals, could she have been lied to about them?

Right after that, I crossed paths with Kim. She too could not confirm the results of the second round of voting nor whether she had even seen them. But a woman next to her, sensing my dismay, said she must have won by a lot. They escaped my further questions through a door.

Now, I wasn't sure what to make of this. There were several possibilities, including but not limited to:

1. Kim had reached 60%—as a result, Kelly decides to concede, either requesting or accepting an offer to make a concession speech in exchange for not having the results shared on the big screen for the delegates
2. Kim had again not eclipsed 60%—a deal is struck where Kelly concedes even though the rules state a third round of voting must occur if no candidate reaches 60%
3. Kelly (or Kelly *and* Kim) were told Kim had won—Kelly decides to concede without verifying whether Kim had indeed reached 60% or not

Any of these three may have occurred, the third being slightly more likely in my opinion based on the fact that Kelly says she did not see the second round results: "I, um, no, because we knew they were good."

Maybe with further conversation with Kim and Kelly or the MN-GOP it can be cleared up what exactly happened, for those of us delegates (and anyone else) that are interested.

I later asked Rep. Eric Lucero what he thought about the MNGOP not showing the results on the big screen. He said that was normal and did not indicate he took issue with it.

Now, it may be how things have been done in the past, but that doesn't make it right. Chair David Haan had stood before the more than two thousand attendees talking about how great the electronic voting equipment was. And not only would they not share the source code nor demonstrate its auditability, but in this case they weren't even going to put the results on the big screen. Someone else suggested to me this was a common face-saving practice for the losing candidate. That was not satisfying to me.

When not many people seemed share my concern about the lack of transparency, my attention to detail was further heightened.

How Much is a Party Endorsement Worth?

I think the overall endorsement process in Minnesota is rife with irregularities which water down the value of endorsements in general, but each endorsement should be evaluated on a case by case basis. For example, candidates like Mark Bishofsky worked really hard to get delegates favorable to him into the process in order to comfortably win his District 33B endorsement. Nathan Wesenberg also educated his base who showed up in strong numbers—although he was stimied with a different tactic to prevent an endorsement from even happening.

Now, I haven't even begun to discuss the unopposed state auditor endorsement, the attorney general endorsement, or the governor endorsement. I have thoughts but I think careful readers will have gotten a feel for what I am paying attention to and a hint at my provisional conclusions.

In the case of secretary of state, I'm not sure what to think. And what may have happened if a third candidate who couldn't be "accommodated" had been given the chance to speak?

Candidates without an endorsement tag may do just fine this year. Natural turnout will be high for a midterm, possibly historic, with independents and democrats voting for republicans in great numbers. Candidates without endorsements, such as Doug Wardlow, will do well in large part because voters are paying much closer attention to detail, having been woken up by the narrative collapses of Covid-19 and the real Big Lie, that somehow the Big Guy surpassed 81 million votes.

Compared with just a year ago, more people are able to read and research open source intelligence (OSINT) and seek the truth with a discerning eye and spirit, not giving up until they find it. They are looking at old questions with fresh eyes and having the wisdom and courage to expect and demand candidates for public office be ready to serve their constituents and not other masters.

On the broader subject of endorsements, my hope is for readers to take not the Party's or another person's word for a candidate's merits, but instead take it upon themselves to ask basic questions about a candidate for public office. Ask and keep asking and you shall receive.

A few questions you might ask: Does the candidate acknowledge the stolen election? Are they truly America First? Do they listen to you when you speak? Do you think they will listen to you once in office? Are they demonstrating real work (not fake credentials) to prove to you they know what they are talking about, are capable of doing the job, and also are taking risks to represent the people in the face of tyranny?

Electronic Voting

David Haan's plea[155] led to the use of electronic voting devices[156] at the convention through a proposed rule change that was voted on using a standing vote, passing by about 85%/15%. Once again, in my opinion, convenience was chosen over accuracy and reliability. When the decision was made, I smiled and nodded to a woman seated across the aisle. So this is the crowd we're in?

> So, if there is any risk to the integrity of the electronic voting system at our convention, it logically would have to be from some delegate or group of delegates in the room. And what conceivable reason would a delegate have to sabotage the balloting since every delegate is pledged to act in support of the Republican Party and to support endorsements? And frankly, if we have concern for that, we have a much bigger problem as a Party than just what kind of balloting we are going to use. If we have delegates who desire the destruction of the Republican Party, they will work to sabotage any kind of voting process we might choose. I refuse to believe we have such people in our midst.

Chair of the MNGOP, David Haan

This after the Chair of the Party in an email days before the convention suggested anyone even asking questions about the electronic devices from the German company, Padgett, were "saboteurs." Prior to the endorsement process, a motion to strike the proposed rule (to use electronic voting devices) was debated. Several speakers spoke for and against the proposed rule prior to a standing vote. Susan Shogren Smith read the Minnesota Constitution regarding the required use of ballots for elections[157], which includes these endorsement elections.

Later, during the endorsement voting rounds, there were no announcements that I recall addressing the reports of the electronic voting device glitches[158]. Sometimes the vote would not send. The device would ask the voter to vote a SECOND time. Does this mean the original vote did not go through? What would have happened if the voter pressed send, put the device in their pocket, and then didn't realize the glitch? Would their original vote have counted?

---

[155]https://www.facebook.com/100078310876790/videos/690779968839417/
[156]https://erikvanmechelen.substack.com/p/electronic-voting-devices-used-at
[157]https://youtu.be/X7dYzfby-Fo
[158]https://www.youtube.com/shorts/uHEjYRGK01s

Or would there be a no-vote or empty vote which the software could designate for another candidate? This last sentence is speculation, but since the source code was not shown to delegates nor were audits of results shared showing individual device IDs and vote numbers, we cannot yet verify whether our votes went through as we desired. It would have been trivial to program a NO VOTE on some percentage of inputs of a given number, just for one example.

Not sure if you can tell, but I'm not a fan of electronic voting equipment. That said, how could these electronic voting device results be verified?

It would have been simple to share a report showing my device number, 413, with my vote, 7, on the screen to verify to me that my vote went through (while keeping my vote secret, since only I knew that my device number was 413).

Even if using the big screen to scroll through the more than 2,000 device IDs and votes took a few minutes, that would be completed well before the 10 minutes negotiation period for candidates to make deals back stage or in their war rooms.

Campaigns should demand audits of every round of every candidate race: secretary of state, attorney general, and governor (there was only 1 candidate for state auditor, so no voting required there). Dr. Neil Shah asked to see audits, but received no response from the MNGOP.

But the MNGOP *should* have provided these reports to every delegate in real time, if they actually cared about election integrity and wanted to model it in their own convention.

At a minimum, this would have quieted down skeptics like me whose distrust grew as I personally experienced and witnessed glitches, heard about at least one device left unattended, and watched for instance Mike Murphy lose about 60 votes between rounds 3 and 4 after taking the lead in round 3, and then about 100 votes between rounds 4 and 5.

No.	Name	Votes	
7	Mike Murphy	665	31.79 %
5	Scott Jensen	658	31.45 %
6	Kendall Qualls	637	30.45 %
8	Paul Gazelka	127	6.07 %
2	Undecided	3	0.14 %
1	No Preference	1	0.05 %
3	No Endorsement	1	0.05 %

Mike Murphy leading in Round 3... before something changed

Were people really swapping their votes *away* from the leading candidate after he'd just taken the lead? Even a prominent house rep speculated about vote shaving when confronted about his vocal support for another candidate—the vote shaving was *the reason* given for his support of a different candidate. How common knowledge was this line of thinking and how grounded was the speculation? My guess is there were more attendees who put themselves in the camp of 'saboteurs' by the end of the weekend than there were at the start.

Primary Election on August 9

I was embarrassed to reflect on the reality that in previous elections I mindlessly voted for the republican candidates but was not involved in helping to choose them. Having seen how the party puts forward candidates, and the myriad influence tactics employed, I am further embarrassed. Why? Because I was duped. I was under a spell.

Now, we have Party-endorsed candidates and unendorsed candidates, establishment-backed and grassroots-supported America First.

The stage is set.

With the context of heightened concern around voting processes and the modern electronic voting system which in Minnesota seems to violate Minnesota Statute 206.57 Subd.6 Required Certification[159] on account of there being no testing lab identified by the EAC to conduct VVSG 2.0 certifications, we are heading into interesting territory.

But what matters more is not *who* wins, but whether the truth wins.

Will the electronic voting systems which tabulate, record, and report our vote totals be trusted? I don't think they can stand up to the pressure. Which is why so far only risk-limiting audits, not audits of the machines themselves nor the cast vote records nor a comparison of those with paper ballots has been done anywhere in Minnesota.

Once everyone recognizes the implications of that, the truth can break out into the open.

But bringing the truth out and then changing how we do things will depend in large part on you.

---

[159] https://www.revisor.mn.gov/statutes/cite/206.57

Chapter Six - Recommendations

"It takes very little talent or creativity to complain about problems. After all, the people directly impacted by a problem, and eventually those indirectly impacted by the problem, feel the weight and consequences stemming from it. When I speak in front of an audience, I need not complain at length about the violations of liberty underway in America, because the people know the personal toll exacted by those who corrupt the foundation of self-government. The audiences come to hear solutions and to commit to action."

—Captain Seth Keshel, Veteran Lesson VII: Leaders Create Solutions[160] (Ten Lessons for Every Day)

"Never tell people how to do things. Tell them what to do and they will surprise you with their ingenuity."

—General George Patton

It is possible to have actual elections that are not controlled by machines or easily exploited by other means.

The simplest way might be to return to hand counting paper ballots in small, manageable precincts[161]. Local control and oversight. That is easy to understand, and implementable right now. There is no reason for county commissioners to wait for further data to come in. The machines in Minnesota are not in compliance with the

---

[160] https://skeshel.substack.com/p/veteran-lesson-vii-leaders-create
[161] https://rumble.com/v15ykkn-precinct-level-voting.html

latest VVSG 2.0 guidelines and therefore violate our election code, Minnesota Statute 206.57 Subd.6 Required Certification[162].

Although I prefer the simplicity and the community involvement (imagine neighbors getting together on election day to count the votes together), but I recognize that hand counting paper is not the only way.

Machines might be used under certain conditions.

Jeffrey O'Donnell says it very well:

"If Americans' votes are to be recorded and counted by machines, every aspect of those machines' operation, configuration, and data must be recorded, immediately available at no cost or administrative burden to citizens and their independent examiners and confirmed 100% accurate through that independent verification. The absence or shortfall of any of those three imperatives (recorded, available, and independently verified) should immediately cause the public to distrust both the purported results from those machines, and also anyone who insists that they accept those results."

Here Jeff describes a possible future where we still use machines but with conditions to increase clarity that the currently less than useless certifications don't have.

Notice, too, that what Jeff prescribes *includes* an audit. That way we don't have to debate whether to have an audit or how to do an audit for 19 months as the 22-month record retention rules loom ever closer.

This approach also jives well with advocates who can't yet stomach the idea of hand counting paper ballots.

But a method to hand counting paper ballots is viable[163] and is described well by Col. Phil Waldron in the Nye County Commission meeting here where the board voted unanimously to move away from electronic voting equipment in their county elections.

---

[162]https://www.revisor.mn.gov/statutes/cite/206.57
[163]https://youtu.be/GBKz1o_VqAE?t=2501

Waldron's description included a method of using a commercial off the shelf (COTS) camera to take a photo of the front and back of each ballot which would be immediately uploaded to the county website and verifiable by each voter through a unique QR code.

Counties and state legislatures around the country will decide how they want to make elections fair again, and possibly to make every voter's vote count for the first time in decades.

It's possible. It's happening. And it could happen in your county.

Will you help to get it done?

Small Counties with Great Potential

22 out of 87 Minnesota counties had fewer than 5,700 votes in 2020 and could perhaps more swiftly move to hand tallying, which is already acceptable by law. These counties could be places to find county commissioners more interested in putting an election integrity item on the agenda during county commissioner board meetings, or even making a courageous decision to pass resolutions to remove electronic voting equipment as seen in Nye County, Nevada and Otero County, New Mexico.

County	Votes
Big Stone	2916
Clearwater	4632
Cook	3699
Grant	3569
Jackson	5693
Kittson	2552
Lac Qui Parle	3974
Lake of the Woods	2375
Lincoln	3058
Mahnomen	2254
Marshall	5016
Murray	4812

County	Votes
Norman	3357
Pipestone	4859
Red Lake	2145
Rock	5139
Stevens	4966
Swift	5100
Traverse	1833
Watonwan	5090
Wilkin	3354
Yellow Medicine	5422

Skeptics might rightly point out that having fair and transparent elections in such small counties wouldn't change the outcomes of larger statewide elections. But we have to start somewhere to inspire change and to say No to tyranny.

Objections to Hand Counting

Time and money.

Time

In a meeting with election officials and commissioners in Morrison County one objection that was raised was the effort involved in hand tallying.

If additional man power is needed to hand count paper ballots in precinct polling places on election day, 204B.195 TIME OFF FROM WORK TO SERVE AS ELECTION JUDGE[164] allows for absence without penalty.

Also, I have met many people who have said they would count the votes for no compensation just so that everyone can regain confidence that the election was conducted fairly and transparently in their precinct and county.

---

[164] https://www.revisor.mn.gov/statutes/cite/204B.195

Minnesota Statute 204C.04 EMPLOYEES; TIME OFF TO VOTE[165] in subdivision 1 already provides the **Right to be Absent** in order to "appear at the employee's polling place, cast a ballot, and return to work on the day of that election, without penalty or deduction from salary or wages because of the absence."

This statute makes mass absentee and mail-in ballots moot.

Money

In the same Morrison County meeting, there was concern that the county was already locked into a rather large contract with the software and hardware vendor. That was a sunk cost if they were to switch to hand tallying. Jeremy Pekula made the point that over time hand counting would be much cheaper and welcomed by the community.

How Much Do Machine Elections Cost?

In earlier chapters we discussed the problems inherent to the ES&S DS200 tabulators that were in use in 65 of 87 Minnesota counties during the 2020 election.

But this was not the only ES&S equipment in play. In 2020, some counties began upgrading to DS450s and DS850s.

---

[165]https://www.revisor.mn.gov/statutes/cite/204C/full

Chapter Six - Recommendations

Connie Kurtzweg

From:	Hoversten, Mike <mahoversten@essvote.com>
Sent:	Friday, March 27, 2020 4:09 PM
To:	Connie Kurtzweg
Cc:	Rice, Trish; Menges, Sheri
Subject:	RE: Election Planning in light of COVID-19

CAUTION: This email was sent from outside of McLeod County. Unless you recognize the sender and know the content, do not click links or open attachments.

Connie,

It was a pleasure to talk to you and your team this morning. I am enclosing the MCCC pricing on the DS450 below. Let me know if you have any questions. I hope you have a nice weekend!

1. DS450 - including shipping, table, two 8GB thumb drives, and one year of warranty. $50,745.00
2. Installation - $1,925.00
3. Training - $1,700.00
4. Ballot Jogger - $750.00
5. Election Day on-site Support - $4,675.00 optional
6. Extra 8GB Thumb Drive - $210.00
7. Post Warranty Hardware Maintenance Silver Agreement - $1,895.00 per year
8. Post Warranty Firmware Agreement - $1,575.00 per year

DS450 Pricing Quote Sent to

While county commissioners in other states have described these machines as being built in Omaha, Nebraska, both the DS450 and DS850 are made in Germany.

Assembled in Germany

These newer models are quite expensive.

McLeod County, Minnesota
MCCC-DS450 Purchase Proposal Quote
Submitted by Election Systems & Software
Purchase Solution Includes:

Item	Description	Quantity	Unit Price	Total
Tabulation Hardware and Optional Items:				
ESS DS450	NEW Model DS450 (Includes Scanner, Steel Table/Cart, Start-up Kit, Dust Cover, Reports Printer, Audit Printer, Battery Backup, Two (2) USB Cables, Two (2) 8GB Thumb Drives, Shipping of the Unit and One (1) Year Warranty)	1	$50,745.00	$50,745.00
Supplies	8GB Thumb Drive (Additional)	1	$210.00	$210.00
Other	Ballot Jogger	1	$750.00	$750.00
Installation	DS450 Installation (1st Unit)	1	$1,925.00	$1,925.00
Equipment Operations Training	Equipment Operations Training - Price is Per One-Day Class (Class size limited to 20 attendees per session.)	1	$1,700.00	$1,700.00
Election Day Support	Election Day Support (One Event includes a person on-site the day before, day of, and day after an election-optional)	1	$4,675.00	$4,675.00
Post-Warranty License and Maintenance and Support Fees:				
Hardware Maintenance and Support:				
HMA DS450	HMA DS450 - Silver Coverage (Maintenance Once Every 24-Months)	1	$1,895.00	$1,895.00
Hardware Maintenance and Support:				
Firmware License	Firmware License - DS450	1	$1,575.00	$1,575.00

Purchase Proposal Quote for McLeod County in 2020

Even the Site Support at $4,250 *alone* could be repurposed toward 20 election judges at $20 an hour for 10 hours. Many more election judges could be hired with the $50,000 spent on the DS450 tabulator. Furthermore, if we legislatively removed or dramatically shortened the absentee and early voting periods, absentee ballot board work would be reduced and the election process further simplified.

Meanwhile, Saint Louis County recently purchased the DS950[166], one of the newest electronic voting machines on the market, likely costing about $250,000.

It's one thing to spend a lot of tax-payer money on vulnerable

---

[166]https://www.essvote.com/products/ds950/

machines, but another to actually use them correctly. For instance, the DS200 Operator Guide[167] is 222 pages long.

The following two emails between staff at ES&S and the County Elections Administrator in McLeod County demonstrate that there is much vendor hand-holding to maintain and operate these machines.

From: Janet Betsinger <Janet.Betsinger@co.mcleod.mn.us>
Sent: Tuesday, August 25, 2020 11:34 AM
To: Rice, Trish <trish.rice@essvote.com>
Cc: Connie Kurtzweg <Connie.Kurtzweg@co.mcleod.mn.us>
Subject: Write-In Programming

Hi Trish,

We are working on the programming for SeaChange and just wanted to verify the Capture Ballot Images section. We are only wanting to capture the Write-in's only, so are we wanting the "Print Write-In Review Report" to be selected to "Don't auto-print", correct? Since this will be our first time utilizing this feature, we just want to be sure that we are requesting the correct programming for the image section. If you could verify that I am on the write page, I would appreciate it.

Capture Ballot Images?:   Write-in's only
                          ○ When polls close
Print Write-in Review Report: ◉ Don't auto-print

Janet Betsinger
Property Tax & Election Administrator
County of McLeod
2391 Hennepin Avenue North
Glencoe, MN 55336
320-864-1203

---

[167] https://www.dropbox.com/s/9tgjadp53l7e34o/ES%26S%20DS%20200%20Operator%20Guide.pdf?dl=0

Connie Kurtzweg

From:	Rice, Trish <trish.rice@essvote.com>
Sent:	Thursday, November 5, 2020 11:21 AM
To:	Connie Kurtzweg
Cc:	Janet Betsinger
Subject:	RE: call please

*** CAUTION: This email was sent from outside of McLeod County. Unless you recognize the sender and know the content, do not click links or open attachments.***

Connie,

Update Election Results Manually
1. From the Update menu, click Update Election Results Manually to open the Update Election Results Manually window.
2. Select the reporting group (Absentee) that you want to update and click OK. The following window appears.
3. Click Precinct or type a precinct identification number in the Precinct number field.
4. Select replace
5. Enter totals – remember you have to include over and under votes
4. Click OK to update your results.

Trish Rice | Account Manager
M: 402.689.5044
trish.rice@essvote.com | www.essvote.com

Election Systems & Software
Attn: Customer Support
11128 John Galt Blvd.
Omaha, NE 68137

Are we asking too much of our election officials at the county level to not only maintain and operate but also mitigate cyber threats to these machines?

The County Commission Strategy

How can these changes actually happen?

County commissioners have concurrent jurisdiction to govern the overall conduct of elections. Ultimately they must decide whether to use electronic voting equipment to begin with and, if they do, whether to certify local elections run on insecure hardware and software. For the time being, only hand counting paper ballots minimizes fraud to the fullest extent.

In this video[168], David Clements, speaking in Rochester on the first night of the MNGOP state convention (at a separate location), describes the county commissioner strategy. Here's my take[169] on the same.

Does it make sense to use the same machines in 2020 again in 2022[170]?

You too can stand in the gap[171].

Resolutions

By having conversations to raise awareness among your county commissioners[172], you can then work toward drafting and passing resolutions.

In addition to resolutions that Rick Weible has provided[173] on MidwestSwampWatch.com, I want to suggest a few that are focused on machines.

Here are a few areas you could focus on:

1. Remove Machines (epollbooks, tabulators, election management systems)
2. Turn on Cast Vote Records (CVRs) in tabulators and tabulation systems

The following are not in resolution form, but I will gladly work with anyone to produce formal resolutions.

Remove Machines

---

[168] https://rumble.com/v15yha1-county-commission-strategy.html
[169] https://rumble.com/v18ouv9-county-commission-strategy-in-minnesota.html
[170] https://www.youtube.com/watch?v=KLGl9uGv0kE
[171] https://www.youtube.com/watch?v=gKZjZMFlj8w
[172] https://youtu.be/KLGl9uGv0kE
[173] https://midwestswampwatch.com/mn-actions

Epollbooks (poll pads), tabulators, and election management systems violate 206.57 Subd.6 Required Certification because the EAC has not designated any testing lab to perform its VVSG 2.0 certifications, and 206.57. Subd.6 requires that voting equipment be in compliance with those standards.

Turn ON Cast Vote Records (CVRs) in tabulators and tabulation systems

Scan Ballot

Use the Scan Ballot option to perform a ballot test for the DS200 and the ballot diverter if you are using a ballot diverter. The results will appear in the **Reports** menu option, located below the **Scan Ballot** menu option.

Note: If the election is set up to save no ballot images, the DS200 will not save any ballot images or cast vote records and the public and protected counters will not increment. This is a feature specifically used for hardware testing and should not be used to validate the tabulator's mark detection accuracy during L&A.

Pg 57 of the DS200 Operator's Manual

No Minnesotan has yet received cast vote record (CVR) reports from any of the 87 counties in the state, even though these reports represent a key element in the machine audit trail. For instance, a comparison of paper ballots with the cast vote record in a precinct would represent a version of a micro-audit. Notice that this comparison is *different* from what post-election reviews are doing, which is comparing the aggregate vote totals (stored in the election management system database and tabulator tapes) with the hand counted ballots. Jeff Lenberg has shown the ability to manipulate the database and the tapes to match[174] while leaving them non-matching with the paper ballots.

Notice that I am focused on the machines. Absentee ballot board balance is important, yes. Removing drop boxes is important, yes. Even with balanced absentee ballot boards, the machines are counting. Even if drop boxes are removed in some areas, mail-in

---

[174]https://rumble.com/vgi89t-hacking-democracy-antrim-county-mi-edition.html

fraud and mule-based fraud will still be simple enough so long as there are *some* drop boxes sprinkled throughout the state. Even if all drop boxes were removed, absentee ballot cheating could still occur. Note that legislation requiring 24-hour surveillance of drop boxes does little to prevent fraud occurring. Once a ballot is in the drop box, it is a legal ballot. See 2000 Mules for proof that 4,000,000 minutes of surveillance footage did next to nothing to preventing ballot traffickers from exploiting this critical weakness in our election system.

Let's get to work.

On June 15, 2022, David Clements' advice[175] was spot on:

"People asking what you can do. Use a search engine. Locate your commissioners' email and phone numbers. Call, write, and show up to your next commission meeting, and support our efforts for transparency. Likewise, find a contact for the SOS and AG's office and give them hell. Stop being a spectator."

Are You a County Commissioner, City Council Member, or Township Supervisor?

Through the concept of "lesser magistrates", the most local officials may be our last defense against overt tyranny.

Help to inspire courage in them by showing your support of their tough decisions ahead, whether to certify local elections run on fraudulent machines.

In a June 20, 2022 township board meeting[176] in Haven Township, Sherburne County, Rick Weible presented his election improvement

---

[175] https://t.me/theprofessorsrecord/7412
[176] https://erikvanmechelen.substack.com/p/supervisor-indicates-that-he-wont

plan[177], focusing on numerous issues discovered throughout Minnesota and Sherburne County.

He began his presentation stressing Minnesota Statute 206.56 Authorization for Use[178].

206.56. Subdivision 1.Municipalities.

The governing body of a municipality, at a regular meeting or at a special meeting called for the purpose, may provide for the use of an electronic voting system in one or more precincts and at all elections in the precincts, subject to approval by the county auditor. The governing body shall disseminate information to the public about the use of a new voting system at least 60 days prior to the election and shall provide for instruction of voters with a demonstration voting system in a public place for the six weeks immediately prior to the first election at which the new voting system will be used.

No system may be adopted or used unless it has been approved by the secretary of state pursuant to section 206.57.

> **206.58 AUTHORIZATION FOR USE.**
>
> Subdivision 1. **Municipalities.** The governing body of a municipality, at a regular meeting or at a special meeting called for the purpose, may provide for the use of an electronic voting system in one or more precincts and at all elections in the precincts, subject to approval by the county auditor. The governing body shall disseminate information to the public about the use of a new voting system at least 60 days prior to the election and shall provide for instruction of voters with a demonstration voting system in a public place for the six weeks immediately prior to the first election at which the new voting system will be used.
>
> No system may be adopted or used unless it has been approved by the secretary of state pursuant to section 206.57.

60 days notice not provided in some townships and counties when new software introduced

Remember Dakota County election official Andy Lokken describing the unique nature of Minnesota? Well, that uniqueness apparently "creates a delay in software getting here."[179]

Those "delays" may have led to a violation of Minnesota Statute

---

[177] https://img1.wsimg.com/blobby/go/47803963-5178-4387-9865-0ea08f5332bd/Election%20Performance%20Improvement%20Plan%2020220602.pdf

[178] https://www.revisor.mn.gov/statutes/cite/206.58

[179] https://www.youtube.com/watch?v=mE1e3XGf7xM

206.58.

For a definition of "Electronic voting system", see 206.56 Subd 8.

> § Subd. 8. **Electronic voting system**. "Electronic voting system" means a system in which the voter records votes by means of marking a ballot, so that votes may be counted by automatic tabulating equipment in the polling place where the ballot is cast or at a counting center.
>
> An electronic voting system includes automatic tabulating equipment; nonelectronic ballot markers; electronic ballot markers, including electronic ballot display, audio ballot reader, and devices by which the voter will register the voter's voting intent; software used to program automatic tabulators and layout ballots; computer programs used to accumulate precinct results; ballots; secrecy folders; system documentation; and system testing results.

Electronic voting system definition, to refer back to 206.56 Subd.1

206.56 Subd. 8.Electronic voting system.

"Electronic voting system" means a system in which the voter records votes by means of marking a ballot, so that votes may be counted by automatic tabulating equipment in the polling place where the ballot is cast or at a counting center.

An electronic voting system includes automatic tabulating equipment; nonelectronic ballot markers; electronic ballot markers, including electronic ballot display, audio ballot reader, and devices by which the voter will register the voter's voting intent; software used to program automatic tabulators and layout ballots; computer programs used to accumulate precinct results; ballots; secrecy folders; system documentation; and system testing results.

> § Subd. 6. **Required certification.** In addition to the requirements in subdivision 1, a voting system must be certified by an independent testing authority accredited by the Election Assistance Commission or appropriate federal agency responsible for testing and certification of compliance with the federal voting systems guidelines at the time of submission of the application required by subdivision 1 to be in conformity with voluntary voting system guidelines issued by the Election Assistance Commission or other previously referenced agency. The application must be accompanied by the certification report of the voting systems test laboratory. A certification under this section from an independent testing authority accredited by the Election Assistance Commission or other previously referenced agency meets the requirement of Minnesota Rules, part 8220.0350, item L. A vendor must provide a copy of the source code for the voting system to the secretary of state. A chair of a major political party or the secretary of state may select, in consultation with the vendor, an independent third-party evaluator to examine the source code to ensure that it functions as represented by the vendor and that the code is free from defects. A major political party that elects to have the source code examined must pay for the examination. Except as provided by this subdivision, a source code that is trade secret information must be treated as nonpublic information, according to section 13.37. A third-party evaluator must not disclose the source code to anyone else.

Required Certification Not Met Under "VVSG 2.0"

In addition to the non-compiance with Minnesota Statute 206.57 Subd.6 Required Certification[180], county commissioners, city coun-

---

[180] https://www.revisor.mn.gov/statutes/cite/206.57

cils, and township supervisors have everything they need statutorily to question the machines, do away with them, or decide to withhold their certification of local elections in either the August 9 primary or the November 8 midterms.

Are You a Candidate?

I am calling on all candidates to speak boldly on election issues in public and in conversations with voters while door knocking.

Even better, urge commissioners to remove machines.

Short of that, help them to pass resolutions so that election officials will turn ON cast vote record (CVR) functionality for the primary on Aug 9, which apparently was turned off in at least some counties in 2020. Else you may not be able to trust the result of your election.

A few more considerations:

- Prepare to challenge results of elections
- Spend a little less than normal on marketing
- Save cash to pay for a discretionary audit[181] for the primary and midterms
- Join fellow citizens at county commissioner meetings (record it and share it with your supporters to inspire them to do the same)

We are in uncharted waters.

These times are not normal.

The primaries are fast approaching. We cannot say "we will get them next time" - this is our time.

---

[181] https://www.sos.state.mn.us/elections-voting/how-elections-work/recounts/

Use Your Platform

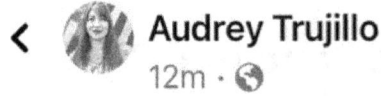

County Commissioners:

I am asking that each commissioner NOT certify the election results for the New Mexico Primary held on June 7th, 2022 until the following has been completed:
CRV (Cast Vote Record) has been provided
Hand re-count has been completed
A forensic audit has been completed
The Commission has the power to request these items and not certify the election results until the election is worthy of certification.

SOS candidate in New Mexico asking commissioners not to certify until conditions are met

I will make similar requests to Trujillo of our commissioners across the state. If you know a commissioner, please let them know. If you are commissioner reading this, thank you. We are already in territory (in other states, like New Mexico) where county commissioners are being put to the test. Are you going to certify your county's primary election on August 9 if it was run on machines that aren't certified according to the latest VVSG 2.0 standards, which may put that equipment in violation of Minnesota Statute 206.57 Subd.6 Required Certification? How about on November 8?

I am also calling for all America First Candidates to make speaking about the election machines a priority. If you don't think machines can alter elections, look at Kandiss Taylor's gubernatorial result in the Georgia primaries. She had 60,000 volunteers but somehow only received 40,000 votes. That's the power of an algorithm to swap votes.

When you're evaluating candidates, consider: If candidates are not speaking about election machines, why aren't they?

Do You Have A Few Minutes Per Day?

Jeffrey O'Donnell recently wrote on his Telegram channel: "Every byte of data we get now is a byte they cannot truly destroy in September. Don't lose sight of that."

Chapter Six - Recommendations

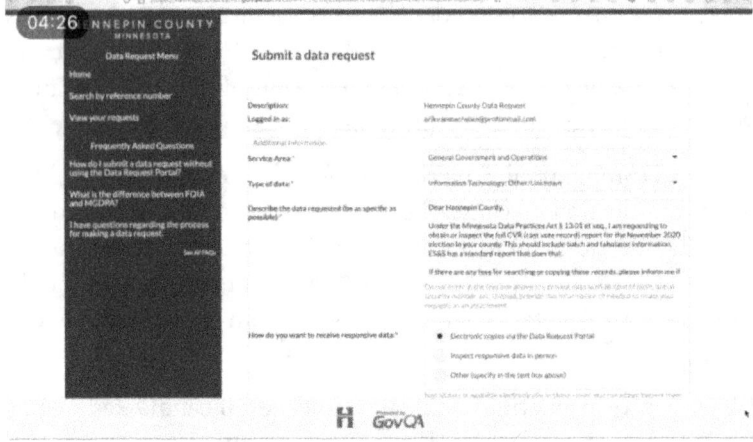

For demo, visit: https://rumble.com/vyy792-foia-request-for-report-of-cast-vote-record-cvr.html

Data Request from Hennepin County

Jeff has provided a general guide to FOIA requests[182].

I also share more about FOIA possibilities on the Erik for SOS channel[183].

Vote in Person in the Primary and Midterm Elections

The Primary Election is on August 9, 2022.

It is important that republicans (and anyone planning to vote for republican candidates) who are supporting America First candidates vote in person on election day, as late in the day as possible.

Even if you join the queue five minutes before polls closed, you are legally allowed to vote, even if the line is very long. The polling place will post someone in the line marking the end of the line at

---

[182]https://magaraccoon.com/foia.html
[183]https://t.me/erikmn

the deadline. Everyone in front of that person already at the polling location in their precinct should be allowed to vote.

Why vote in person late in the day?

Because we now have reason to believe that there are centralized mechanisms that through a combination of the statewide voter registration system, the epollbooks, and the scanned barcode when absentee ballots are delivered which allow the powers that be to see the full landscape of who has voted and who has not.

If the vast majority of republican voters vote very late in the day, say at 5pm or later, then it becomes increasingly difficult to cheat using illegitimate absentee ballots. (I use the word illegitimate because by statute once a ballot enters the system it is by definition legal.)

Therefore, I am urging republican voters *not* to take the convenient option and vote through absentee or early voting.

If you are in a mail-in ballot precinct, you have the option to deliver your mail-in ballot directly to the county clerk up until 3pm on election day (according to Minnesota Statute 203B.08[184]).

Are you an event planner? Imagine holding a post-election party for republicans nearby the polling place to gather after voting in person to encourage reluctant in-person republican voters to take this small action step for election integrity.

Of course, voting in person doesn't prevent tabulator vote-swapping or server-based tampering, but it does force those attempting to subvert our elections to resort to electronic methods at greater scale, which is risky.

Finally, considering sharing this book[185] with your elected officials, candidates, and county commissioners to provide context on the depth of the problem we're facing, and what they can do about it.

---

[184] https://www.revisor.mn.gov/statutes/cite/203B.08
[185] https://leanpub.com/sim2020

Chapter Seven - Security Threats to Our Election System

"The end game of all this electronic record manipulation is the vote tally. The consequence of a compromised vote tally is the selection of a compromised public official. Vote tallies can be manipulated in a variety of ways. Bad actors can program tabulators to automatically shift a percentage of votes from one candidate to another when the tabulator reads a scanned ballot image and allocates votes in a vote tally database. The tabulation databases themselves can be directly manipulated to replace actual vote tallies with alternative vote tallies. Bad actors who have access to vote tallies before election precincts close can use that information to know if they need to stuff the ballot box with more ballots than anticipated."

—Patrick Colbeck, in *The 2020 Coup*

The following is an excerpt from Chapter 3 of *The 2020 Coup* by Patrick Colbeck[186].

Election Infrastructure Components

Let's delve into a discussion of the security threats to our election system. Rather than provide you with a list of the risks that I have discovered on my own, I believe it would be quite revealing to hear from people who investigated these risks prior to the 2020 general election and who now assert that it was the most secure election in American history.

---

[186] https://www.amazon.com/2020-Coup-What-Happened-Can/dp/1955043655

An investigative news story by NBC News that aired on January 10, 2020, provided a stark summary of the hacking risks for voting systems connected to the internet.

CYNTHIA MCFADDEN: We've heard it at congressional hearings for years.

MR. HICKS: Our voting machines are not connected to the internet.

KEVIN SKOGLAN: We knew that wasn't true.

CYNTHIA MCFADDEN: Cybersecurity expert Kevin Skoglan wanted to prove it so he and nine other independent security consultants created their own search engine looking for election systems online.

KEVIN SKOGLAN: We found over 35 had been left online and we continue to find more.
[...]

CYNTHIA MCFADDEN: Skoglan's team found ES&S voting systems online in at least some of the precincts in 11 states including the battleground states of Florida, Michigan and Wisconsin.

If you were able to get inside these systmes, could you do more than perhaps mess up the preliminary results, could you actually get deeper in the system?

KEVIN SKOGLAN: Absolutely. And that's my biggest concern.

On July 28, 2020, three months before the November 3 election, the Cybersecurity & Infrastructure Security Agency (CISA), the agency responsible for understanding, managing, and reducing the risk to our cyber and physical infrastructure, released what they referred to as a Critical Infrastructure Security and Resilience Note, which included a list of election components vulnerable to cyber and non-cyberattacks. These components are the fundamental building blocks of our election system. Let's look at what CISA identified as vulnerable components.

Voter Registration Database

The first of these vulnerable building blocks is the voter registration database. Voter registration is an ongoing process to create new records, update existing records, and remove outdated records. Voter registration databases receive data automatically and indirectly from a variety of sources, including other government agencies and organizations that aid in the registration process. The databases contain information on whether people are entitled to vote, where they can vote, and on what unique ballot style they will vote, based upon voter geographical placement within multiple layers of political and taxing districts. The management of voter registration databases are the responsibility of each state. These databases are typically managed by the secretary of state for each state. These databases are used to enter, store, and edit voter registration information. Security risks include servers that host the database and online portals that provide access. Since these databases are connected to the internet, they pose serious security risks due to the ability for them to be hacked.

Pollbooks

Another vulnerable building block of the election system are pollbooks. Pollbooks are precinct-specific extracts of the statewide voter registration files. Poll workers use the information in the pollbooks to determine whether or not a voter is eligible to vote. It contians information used to validate the identity of a prospective voter. When voters vote in person at the polls, poll workers use this information to decide whether or not the voter is eligible to receive a ballot to cast at that precinct. Poll workers also use this information to validate the identity of an absentee voter before allowing the absentee ballot to be tabulated. Pollbooks may be either networked or non-networked. Networked pollbooks are electronic pollbooks with a connection to an external database such as the statewide voter registration file. Non-networked pollbooks are either paper pollbooks or digital files saved on local computers. Either way, poll workers use pollbooks to validate the identity and eligibility of prospective voters. Poll workers are also empowered to view, edit, and modify voter records via the pollbooks. Pollbook integrity is critical. The information which they contain determines whether a voter receives a ballot or doesn't.

Ballot Preparation
Ballots are another key election infrastructure component with security vulnerabilities. Modern ballots are much more sophisticated than a piece of paper with checkboxes next to names. Today's ballots are sophisticated paper and/or digital documents. In fact, in some cases, ballots are replaced by Direct-Recording Electronic (DRE) voting machines.

Ballot preparation is a complicated process of overlaying political geographies with the contests and candidates specific to each district and then translating those layouts into unique combinations of ballot data. Ballot preparation data takes multiple forms such as ballot images (both paper and electronic), the data files necessary to build ballot images, audio files for special use ballots, and specific files for export to external systems such as websites for Uniformed and Overseas Citizens Absentee Voting Act (UOCAVA)-focused digital systems. Ballot preparation also generates the data necessary for tabulating votes within a voting machine and aggregating tabulated votes within a jurisdiction or state. This process is usually completed in an election documents and records management system (EDRMS), which is special software designed to manage documents and records throughout the document lifecycle, from creation to destruction. Access to the information in such systems would enable anyone attempting to subvert the integrity of an election with the information necessary to create ballots independently of election officials. Of course, ballots are also where voters record their votes. Vote tallies are generated from the information on ballots therefore their integrity is very important to protect.

Voting Machines
Another class of election infrastructure components that are at risk are voting machines. Voting machine systems consist of the technol-

ogy and processes used to cast and, in some cases, generate voter ballots of all types (paper-based or digital systems such as DRE voting). Voting machines often feature ballot marking capabilities that assist in providing an audit trail although DRE systems are noteworthy for their lack of paper audit trail. Electronic voting machines feature hardware and software components which must be certified as "secure" prior to use in an election. The Federal Election Assistance Commission provides a list of certified voting system configurations. Election equipment is supposed to be delivered in a configuration consistent with a certified configuration. The process of preparing electronic voting machines includes loading the ballot files created during ballot preparation onto the voting machines' software. Voting machines are held in storage in the custody of election officials, but after delivery they are placed at voting locations for use during early voting and on Election Day. Voting machines are the most visible form of technology that voters interact with during the voting process.

Tabulation Systems

Tabulators are critical election infrastructure components with significant security vulnerabilities. At the precinct level, tabulators are used to read a ballot, convert the ballot image to votes, and add the vote data on a given ballot the running tally of votes stored in a digital table. Precinct-level vote tallies are then aggregated by centralized vote tabulation systems at the municipal, county, and state levels. Collectively, these systems help determine and communicate the results of an election. If tabulators are compromised, they can shift votes from one candidate to another. These vote shifts can change the results of an election.

Official Websites

Official websites are additional critical components of election infrastructure used by election officials to communicate information to the public, including how to register to vote, where to vote, and to convey election results. Sometimes election websites are hosted on government-owned infrastructure, but they often are hosted by commercial partners. Whether hosted by the government, commercially, or privately, websites can be areas of vulnerability as they often feature network connections to election results databases.

Storage Facilities

Physical buildings, such as storage facilities, polling places, and election offices, are also critical infrastructure components which need to be secured. Storage facilities may be located on public or private property and may be used to store election and voting system infrastructure before Election Day. Polling places (including early voting locations) are where individuals cast their votes. They may be physically located on public or private property. Election offices are where election officials conduct official business. These offices can be in public libraries, municipal buildings, private homes, and public areas for jurisdictions without a dedicated workspace.

Summary

Today's modern electronic voting system has quite a few moving parts. The more complex the system, the more vulnerable it is to exploitation. Furthermore, many election officials do not have the technical expertise regarding information technology to mitigate the risks to these systems. Of particular concern is the trend toward increasing network connectivity between election components. The centralization of our election system by networking components together makes it easier for fewer and fewer bad actors to subvert integrity of the election system. Manual systems featuring paper ballots eliminate many of the security vulnerabilities inherent with electronic voting systems. Election officials, poll workers, and poll challengers can see, touch, and feel paper-based election systems. They can secure these systems by observation. In contrast, it is very difficult for these same individuals to monitor electronic communications.

Consequences of Election Infrastructure Security Breaches

The consequences of security breaches according to CISA fall into the following three impact categories: confidentiality, integrity, and availability impacts. The most significant of these, of course, pertain to the integrity of election results.

The integrity of our election systems can be subverted in a variety of ways. While election integrity has always been a concern, our modern electronic voting systems make it easier than ever to effect large scale changes with minimum effort. Key Election records such as our statewide voter registration file, the pollbooks, the ballot itself, and the subsequent vote tallies have all been digitized in our modern election system. Each of these records are connected in what can be described as our election record chain of custody.

Each record in the election record chain of custody can be thought of as a link. The first link is the statewide voter registration file. The statewide voter registration file contains a list of everyone eligible to vote and includes information necessary to verify the identity of voters such as their drivers license signature. The next link is that of the pollbook. The pollbooks are simply precinct-specific extracts of the statewide voter registration file used by poll workers to verify the identity of a given voter prior to processing a ballot cast in the voter's name. That makes ballots the next link in the election record chain of custody. The ballot, of course, contains the intended votes of a voter. The final link in the chain of custody is the vote tally. The vote tally should simply be the sum of all the votes cast on valid ballots.

If you break any single link in the chain, you break the integrity of the entire election. For example, if you have an incorrect birthdate in the statewide voter registration file, it will propagate to an incorrect birthdate in the pollbooks. If an incorrect birthdate is in the pollbook, someone may receive a ballot despite not having met the minimum age requirement to vote. If an ineligible voter casts a ballot, the subsequent vote tally is compromised.

In a modern electronic voting system, each of the above handoff is digitized. Whereas data transfers or modifications of these records could be easily monitored by any citizen when our elections were driven by paper records, the monitoring of our digital election records is often restricted to a select few. In this light, the push to digitize our election system has severely impaired transparency. As transparency dissolves, so does the integrity of our elections.

How could these links be compromised? Let's start by looking at the statewide voter registration database. Nefarious actors can add, delete, or modify voter registration data in statewide voter registration files. Such actions can enable what are called phantom voters or result in the denial of voting rights to individuals otherwise qualified to vote. The seeding of the statewide voter registration file with "phantom voters" yields a "slush fund" of voters that could be fraudulently assigned to ballots.

If the statewide voter registration file has been corrupted, any pollbooks generated from this database will also be corrupted. This corruption of voter data can go both ways. If bad actors were to access electronic pollbooks, the pollbooks could be used to push fraudulent data to the statewide voter registration file. Furthermore, pollbooks could be accessed real-time by bad actors to reveal who has not yet voted or tap into a voter slush fund. These voter slush funds can be used by clandestine ballot factories to match manufactured ballots to low propensity voters. This matchmaking exercise helps to avoid an abundance of embarrassing "you already voted" remarks by poll workers when a low propensity voter actually shows up at a voting precinct in person to vote.

Ballot integrity can also be compromised. Some modern voting systems use what is referred to as DRE or Direct-Recording Electronic voting machines. Without significant transparency provisions that would compromise the principle of a secret ballot, voters have no substantive assurance that the votes they cast on a voting machine touch screen are actually what has been recorded in the vote tally. Even when paper ballots are used, they can be manipulated to compromise the integrity of the election record chain of custody. Something as simple as the formatting of paper ballots can be used to manipulate elections results. Ballot formatting can be manipulated to trigger scanner errors. These scanner erros in turn will trigger manual or automated adjudication processes. These adjudication processes can then be used to shift votes between candidates. Absentee ballots are particularly vulnerable to this method of subversion as the control over how a vote is cast when there is a scanner error is turned over to poll workers not the voter.

The end game of all this electronic record manipulation is the vote tally. The consequence of a compromised vote tally is the selection of a compromised public official. Vote tallies can be manipulated in a variety of ways. Bad actors can program tabulators to automatically shift a percentage of votes from one candidate to another when the tabulator reads a scanned ballot image and allocates votes in a vote tally database. The tabulation databases themselves can be directly manipulated to replace actual vote tallies with alternative vote tallies. Bad actors who have access to vote tallies before election precincts close can use that information to know if they need to stuff the ballot box with more ballots than anticipated.

If election components are connected to each other on local networks or via internet connections, pollbook ballot tallies and tabulator ballot counts are vulnerable to being re-synchronized with each other to cover any discrepancies between the number of voters and the number of votes cast. If bad actors wish to give the appearnace of a secure election, the total number of voters haded ballots per the pollbook records must reconcile with the number of ballots stored in ballot containers as well as the total number of votes in the final statement of votes.

This is just a small sample of the way security breaches can affect elections.

For those who assert that the 2020 general election was the most secure election in history, ask yourselves which of the security concerns raised by CISA, a federal agency, were addressed between the release of the aforementioned CISA Critical Infrastructure Security and Resilience Note on July 28, 2020, and November 3, 2020.

While the federal government has the authority to identify and mitigate any national secuirty threats to our election system, the US Constitution clearly specifies that state governments are responsible for the conduct of our elections. It is each state's responsibility to ensure that elections are conducted in a secure manner.

In Michigan, one of the 2020 battleground states, the Michigan Election Security Advisory Commission was also tasked with the identification and mitigation of election threats. Their report, issued in October of 2020, identified several significant election security risks. On the topic of the voter registration system, they cited issues with security credential management and a lack of monitoring of suspicious activities. On the topic of post-election audits, they cited a lack of transparency about the process and asserted that the current post-election audit standards did not satisfy the constitutional right of Michigan citizens to conduct an audit of statewide election results. They also cited the threats posed by misinformation or disinformation campaigns, election night reporting risks, and the risks inherent in submitting electronically unofficial election results to county clerks. The report noted that connecting tabulators to the internet or other external networks creates significant risks to the integrity of the election.

For those who assert that the 2020 general election was the most secure election in history, which of the concerns raised in the October report by the Michigan Election Security Advisory Commission were addressed prior to November 3?

Does anyone truly believe that any of these concerns were addressed at all prior to the election?

If not, is it fair to say that there were significant threats to election integrity that were not addressed prior to the November 3, 2020, election?

Paperbacks of the full book by Patrick Colbeck are available on Amazon[187].

---
[187] https://www.amazon.com/2020-Coup-What-Happened-Can/dp/1955043655

Chapter Eight - Where We Go From Here

"After we kick electronic voting systems out of our country, and go back to all-paper, one-day elections - we need to make Election Day a national holiday. It needs to be a holiday not for convenience or to make sure everyone has time to get to the polls. It needs to be a holiday so that once a year we will remember how Americans defeated tyranny within our borders for a second time. That we reaffirmed that our rights come from our Creator and our liberty is a responsibility. And under that framework our government derives its powers only from the consent of the governed."

—Erin Clements[188]

"They don't like playing defense. They don't know how to play defense."

—Gregg Phillips

"Are you ready?"

"Yes."

—From a conversation between Mark Cook and the author at the close of Day 3 of Mike Lindell's Cyber Symposium

---

This is my seventeenth year living in Minnesota, although my family returned to Stevens County each year in my youth from Texas, Gabon, Louisiana, Indonesia, and China, where my dad's work as a geophysicist brought us. In 5th grade and 7th grade (as

---

[188] https://t.me/NewMexicoAuditForce/2205

secretary) I served in the student council, and was later named or voted captain of several sports teams, including my college soccer team which went to the NCAA tournament. After college, I worked four years in the inventory and software divisions at Target in Minneapolis before investing in myself as a freelance writer for the past eight years. I've assisted governors with a USA Today article and a military veteran with his autobiography, cowrote several books, one a Wall Street Journal bestseller, and helped about 90 authors choose the title of their book.

With a growing understanding of what happened on November 3rd, 2020, life took a turn. After working with grassroots Minnesotans seeking audits, I attended Mike Lindell's Cyber Symposium in Sioux Falls, South Dakota in August 2021. There I met people like Draza Smith, Seth Keshel, Mark Cook, and Col. Phil Waldron and also learned from people like Col. Shawn Smith, Patrick Colbeck, Joe Oltmann, and Professor David Clements. Here in Minnesota, I've continued to absorb much from people like Rick Weible and Susan Smith, as well as from those attending county commissioners meetings in Crow Wing, Morrison, Dakota, Wright and Sherburne County.

These experiences and relationships were vital in preparing me to not only make the decision to run for secretary of state in Minnesota, but also to become the servant leader necessary to resolve our election problems, preserve election integrity, and restore confidence to all Minnesota voters that their constitutional right to vote (and to not be disenfranchised of that right) is fully protected.

Outside of learning about elections, I enjoy running, gardening, and playing the piano.

Hebrews 12:1 (KJV) reads "Wherefore seeing we also are compassed about with so great a cloud of witnesses, let us lay aside every weight, and the sin which doth so easily beset us, and let us run with patience the race that is set before us."

What Diplomacy Teaches

A decent amount of my preparation for 2022 actually occurred starting around age 16 when I was introduced by my history teacher in Houston, Texas, to Diplomacy, a tabletop game designed by Allan B. Calhamer, apparently played by JFK and other statesmen[189] and was popularized by play by mail throughout Europe in the Sixties.

I enjoyed the game so much that I formed a club at my high school and later wrote this book[190] and recorded an audiobook[191].

Many of the tactics, tricks, and maneovers I've witnessed this past year I first observed or experienced playing this board game. Other games like weiqi (Go) have furthered my abstract study of war, but Diplomacy's simultaneous movement and lack of imperfect information turned out to be good practice for many interactions and communications of late.

In Diplomacy, as per the rules, cheating is allowed and there are no penalties for cheating. No verbal commitments or written contracts are binding. There are infamous stories[192] of players threatening to broadcast personal secrets about their opponents if they don't agree to do what they want.

In a game with no rules against foul play, the players, including your friends who you've invited to the game, may lie to your face to gain an advantage. They may agree to help you and then help your neighbor instead.

On the surface, the game prepares one to detect liars and subtle deceptions. It teaches one to ask good questions. To listen well. It also tempts one to take what one has not earned. It teaches you that

---

[189]https://www.reddit.com/r/AskHistorians/comments/ifxjnv/do_we_know_if_jfk_or_kissinger_actually_played/
[190]https://www.amazon.com/Diplomacy-Conversations-Erik-van-Mechelen-ebook/dp/B07ZZMVCGR/
[191]https://www.amazon.com/Diplomacy-Conversations-Face-Face-Tournaments/dp/B08742MPJJ/
[192]http://www.diplomacy-archive.com/god.htm

it does not feel good to stab your friend in the back, even if the game allows it and even incentivizes it.

It also teaches patience and attention to detail.

Narratives and alliances and strategic movements must sometimes be developed carefully over a handful of game years (one to two hours)—one wrong move, mistep, or miscalculation can undo that preparation or end the game for you. In one game, I'd carefully for about two hours prepared a coordinated move only to misorder (write the wrong moves), costing me the game.

A single game can sometimes last six hours or longer. In a tournament it's common to play more than one game in a day. Endurance is required.

Rare in tabletop board games, things can even get physical.

In a high stakes moment during a tournament game in Chicago in 2019, I was physically pushed as I requested a conversation from a player who was beginning to work with me but whom another player wanted to keep under his wing.

I decided not to complain.

Later I noticed the man who pushed me went to let the tournament organizer know what happened. That's what was supposed to happen from a sportsmanship perspective, even in a game where the rules specifically state there are no rules. (Therefore, house rules have to be developed by game hosts, leagues, and tournament organizers.)

In short, Diplomacy could well be part of the training to become a politician. Except, in my case, I don't want to be a politician. In his book Zero to One, Peter Thiel described politicians as people who sell themselves. Instead of a politician, I want to be a *public servant*, an elected official completely accountable to the people of Minnesota, the constitution, and to God. I know this is the intent of many others who have stepped up this year. But not everyone.

Don't let endorsements replace your critical thinking. A lot of people trusted Dr. Fauci's endorsement of various protocols and treatments who now regret substituting their God-given ability to think (and intuit) for a man's misguided opinion, to put it lightly.

Don't make this mistake with regard to supporting candidates. Even if your chosen candidate loses or their election is actually a machine (s)election, at least you will have not put your energy and effort into someone who doesn't share your convictions.

It is usually quite simple to tell the difference between someone who is sincere about saving our state and country and someone who isn't.

Fortunately, this year it is easier than ever to recognize whether a candidate is truly America First. Have they consistently said the election was stolen? Do they boldly speak the truth on the basic constitutional topics like gun rights, medical freedom, and CRT? Are they willing to respond to tough questions? And maybe most important: Have they already been working toward the outcomes they say they want to continue working on once in office? What tangible proof can they show of those efforts?

The power of your words and decisions are not to be underestimated. When you make discoveries, share them. Word of mouth spreads quickly.

If discerning the truth and speaking boldly do not come naturally to you, be not afraid and keep practicing. As President Trump said, "Never, ever, give up."

This is an information war.

All hands on deck.

It's time for us to go on the offense.

The Power of Information

Without access to information, how can the public react?

When I was introduced to Andrei, the creator of Project Apario part way through 2021, I began a journey of becoming a better researcher. I was seeking the truth, in large part through our conversations and also through his creation, a research utility called Project Apario.

At the 6m30s mark of the Standing in the Gap movie[193], which you should buy from standinginthegapfilm.com to support it, you'll notice footage that the creator of Project Apario, Andrei Merlescu, created, where the mainstream media is presented in a video and audio montage repeating "a threat to our democracy."

Video created by Andrei

Q post #3614[194] also referred to Andrei's twitter account (where he posted that video), calling it "Information Warfare".

Since that time, Andrei built Project Apario[195], which is a truth

---
[193]https://standinginthegapfilm.com/
[194]https://qalerts.app/?q=3614
[195]https://projectapario.com

repository for declas and FOIA for We the People, built single-handedly and 100% owned by Andrei, no big tech, he owns and manages the stack and has completely secured it.

He has even turned down funding three times.

I've known Andrei about a year and he has not wavered from his mission to make information available to the public so that we can react. There's a mystery that our governments have hidden from us that is discoverable in the JFK files, ordered to be released by President Trump, which the National Archives made UNsearchable but which Project Apario makes searchable.

I have a feeling that Project Apario will host many of the declassified files which come into the public consciousness in the weeks and months and years to come.

Give it a try and support the project if you find value in it.

What you may find instead is a completely different way of learning.

Chapter Nine - A Brief History of Voting Machines and Certifications

In the first place, how did we get to using machines, and *electronic* voting machines, in elections?

Before voting machines, voting was often done by voice throughout the 1800s. Kentucky used voice voting until 1891. The first paper ballots arrive in the early 19th century.

Then came voting machines: first lever, then punch cards.

Lever voting machines have been around a long time.

Chapter Nine - A Brief History of Voting Machines and Certifications

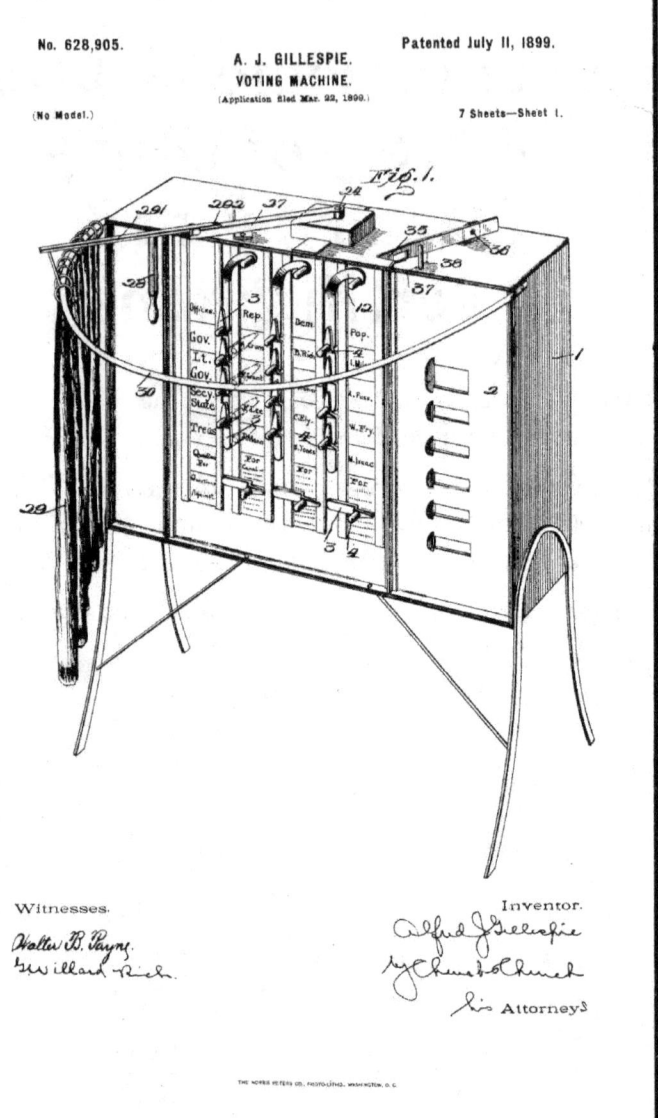

Drawing of Voting Machine

Here's a physical example:

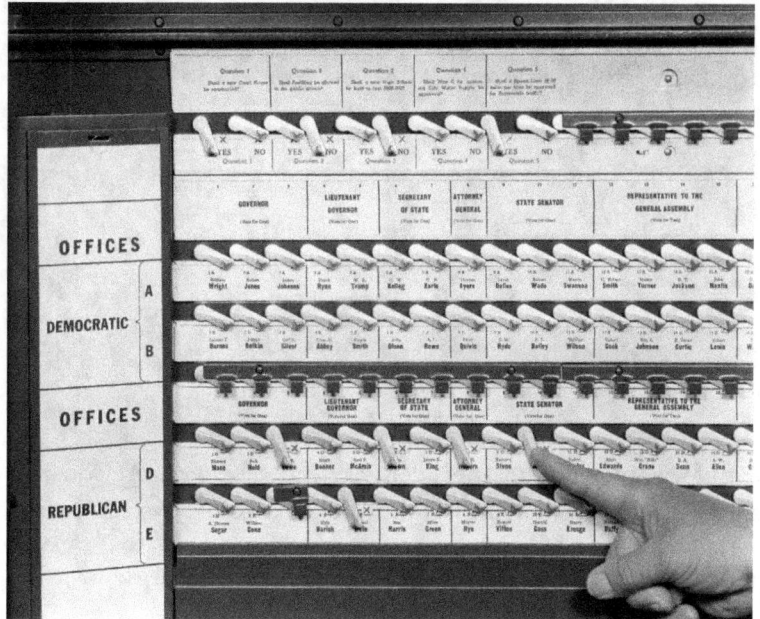

Lever Voting Machine

Punch card systems were developed in the 1960s and were last used in two Idaho counties in 2014, on the Votomatic[196] provided by ES&S.

---
[196]https://verifiedvoting.org/election-system/ess-votomatic/

Chapter Nine - A Brief History of Voting Machines and Certifications

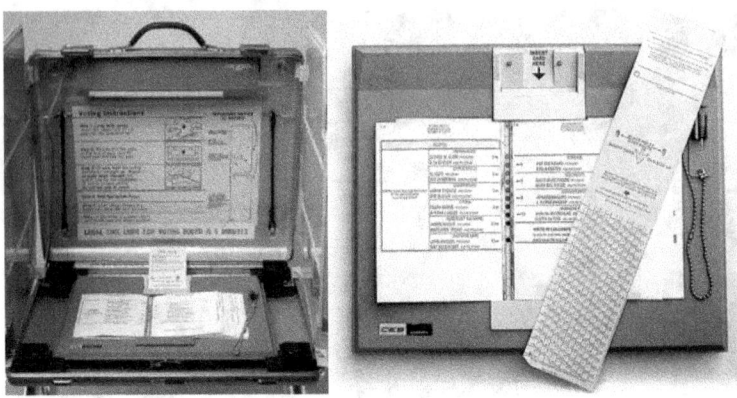

Punch Card System

Fast forward to the 2000 presidential election between Al Gore and George W. Bush. Hanging chads on Sequoia Voting Systems punch-card voting system led to a recount, which Bush won.

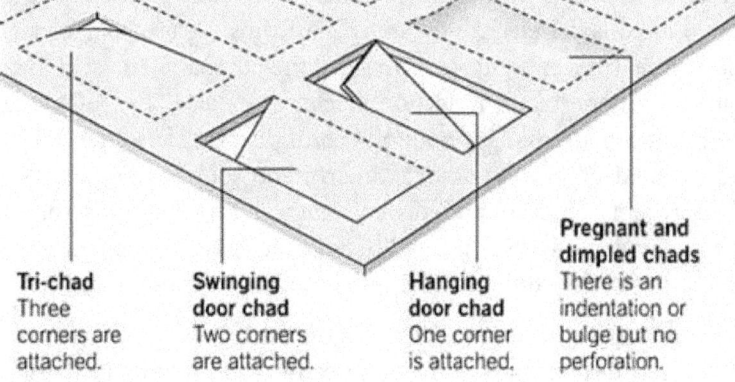

Hanging Chads

Sequoia Voting Systems got its start in the 1970s as Mathematical Systems Corporation of Anaheim, California, offering an alternative to ES&S's Votomatic punch cards. On March 8, 2005 Smartmatic Corp. (a Venezuelan company) acquired Sequoia. This raised eyebrows since Smartmatic had only the previous year been selected to by the Chavez-era Venezuelan government to provide voting systems for the presidential recall election, its first time providing machines[197] for an election. Since June 4, 2010, Smartmatic's parent company has been Dominion Voting Systems.

Dan Sundin summarizes Smartmatic well:

"Smartmatic was founded in 1998 by three Venezuelans, Antonio Mugica, Alberto Anzola, and Roger Pinate. Initially they developed ATMs in Mexico, but the U.S. presidential election in 2000 led the group to consider electronic voting platforms. Venezuelan strongman Hugo Chavez's government gave the company an early loan and its first contract for election machines in 2004. The following year, Smartmatic bought Sequoia Voting Systes, but after a U.S. Department of Justice inquiry, Smartmatic sold Sequoia in 2007. More recently, Smartmatic has become a political lighting rod in the Philippines, with some politicians accusing the company of marketing faulty equipment and orchestrating election fraud."

Back to 2000. According to Sequoia's own employees, Sequoia may have been responsible[198] for the defective punch cards in Florida which led to "hanging chads" or undervotes to the tune of 10,000 in Palm Beach County.

One of Sequoia's workers told[199] Dan Rather:

"My own personal opinion was the touch screen voting system wasn't getting off the ground like that they—like they would hope. And because they weren't having any problems with paper ballots. So, I feel like they—deliberately did all this to have problems with the paper ballots so the electronically voting systems would get off the ground—and which it did in a big way."

Specifically, USC 52 Ch. 209 Subchapter I—PAYMENTS TO STATES FOR ELECTION ADMINISTRATION IMPROVEMENTS AND REPLACEMENT OF PUNCH CARD AND LEVER VOTING MA-

---

[197] https://ia801704.us.archive.org/34/items/smartmatic-sequoia-and-venezuela/Smartmatic%20Sequoia%20and%20Venezuela.pdf

[198] https://web.archive.org/web/20070928013625/http://www.votetrustusa.org/index.php?option=com_content&task=view&id=2560&Itemid=51

[199] https://web.archive.org/web/20070928013625/http://www.votetrustusa.org/index.php?option=com_content&task=view&id=2560&Itemid=51

CHINES. §20902 states: Replacement of punch card or lever voting machines.

Sequoia benefitted from the passage of federal legislation in 2002—the Help America Vote Act of 2002[200]—because *they manufactured electronic voting equipment.*

In 2003 Beverly Harris found Diebold's source code[201] on the internet. Diebold had only entered the elections business a year prior through its purchase of Global Elections Systems, a touch-screen voting technology producer in Texas. The source code revealed that Diebold voting systems used an unsecured access database, meaning anyone could access, change data, and erase logs.

In 2007 Diebold Election Systems rebranded as Premier Election Solutions and in 2009 they sold to Election Systems & Software (ES&S), which by 2014 was the largest manufacturer of United States voting machines (and still used in the majority of Minnesota counties).

The Source Code Review of the Diebold Voting System[202] was published by 6 authors on July 20, 2007, showed the system was 1) vulnerable to malicious software, 2) susceptible to viruses, 3) failed to protect ballot secrecy, and 4) vulnerable to malicious insiders.

More recently, one of the authors of the Diebold review, J. Alex Halderman of Princeton University, provided the Halderman Declaration[203] on Georgia's ballot marking devices (BMD). Halderman has also issued a sealed 25,000-word report[204] on voting systems vulnerabilities.

In an emergency meeting in Otero County, New Mexico in May 2022, nation-state vulnerability expert Jeff Lensberg provided fur-

---

[200] https://www.justice.gov/crt/help-america-vote-act-2002
[201] https://www.computerworld.com/article/2547648/diebold-source-code-leaked-again.html
[202] https://jhalderm.com/pub/papers/diebold-ttbr07.pdf
[203] https://www.documentcloud.org/documents/21038844-20210802-expert-rebuttal-declaration-of-j-alex-halderman
[204] https://libertysword.com/expert-hackers-25000-word-secret-report-threatens-to-uncover-georgias-real-election

ther vulnerabilities[205], some of which he'd uncovered previously in the Antrim County, Michigan investigation. Of particular concern was his vote switching demonstration[206].

Putting the History in Context

The history of voting machines spans over 100 years. However the use of electronic voting machines is very short, only two to three decades. During almost the entirety of that duration, the electronic systems have been shown to be insecure, hackable, and manipulable, sometimes if not often by design.

If access can be gained, whether remotely, over a network, or through the internet, and once inside the machines or databases are configured to be manipulable, then there is ample room for subversion. Even if internet connectivity could be proven not to occur (it has been shown to have occurred), should citizens trust machines that have disturbing baked-in features?

The lack of certifications (and the uselessness of certifications) of voting machines is further troubling.

In the Tarrant County, TX, in the first half of 2022, [:

"...And for the people who said well, the machines are certified, I would say, the space shuttle Columbia was also certified for flight. How'd that turn out? The Boeing 737 Max was certified for passenger operations, and then crashed killing over 500 people in two separate accidents before they finally let experts take a look at it. And my point in saying that is not to try to scare people, but just to say that based on my experience, and I'm not a cyber professional, but I work with cyber pros, and I know the difference between somebody who knows cyber and somebody who doesn't. And if you don't know the difference, then you're in very dangerous

---

[205] https://www.youtube.com/watch?v=Fg6Gf6QjqGM&t=939s
[206] https://www.mixonium.com/public/post/11555

territory when you try to make any conclusions or try to listen to someone who doesn't really know what they're talking about.

"Our voting systems from my perspective based on the expert examiner's report, cannot be trusted with our election. And what they require in order to for you to verify for yourself is that you become a cyber expert. Otherwise, you're forced to trust other people who say they're experts, people who have conflicts of interest, and people who've been trained essentially by the National Association of Secretaries of State, the election directors, and the Election Assistance Commission..."

Certifications Are Less Than Useless

Throughout its certification process[207], the Election Assistance Commission (EAC) which was established by the Help America Vote Act[208] (2002) has *not* certified about 95% of Minnesota counties.

Those county's electronic voting equipment are merely certified by the Minnesota Secretary of State. The few counties that are EAC certified have the problem indicated by Col. Shawn Smith, that those certifications provide the illusion of security when in fact those systems are anything but ready to run secure elections, and by the EAC certificate's own language not an endorsement of the products.

Let's take a look at the certification maps. Remember, being certified or not certified doesn't guarantee system security, as we shall discuss shortly.

In the following image, Red = Certified | White = Not Certified

---

[207] https://www.eac.gov/voting-equipment/system-certification-process
[208] https://www.eac.gov/about_the_eac/help_america_vote_act.aspx

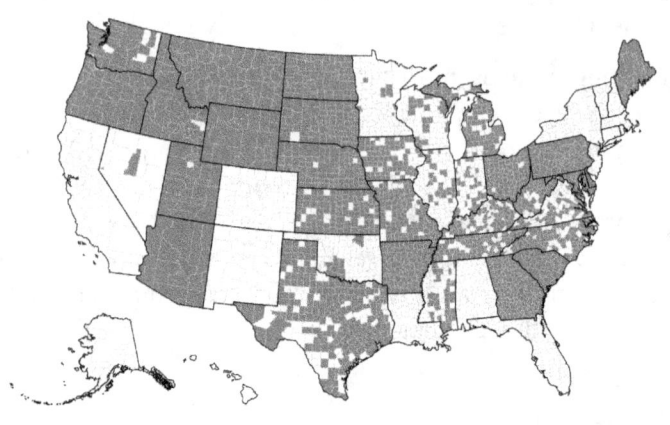

USA EAC Certification Map

If we zoom in on Minnesota, we find that only 6 of 87 counties have voting equipment that is certified by the EAC. Remember, red counties are certified, white are not certified.

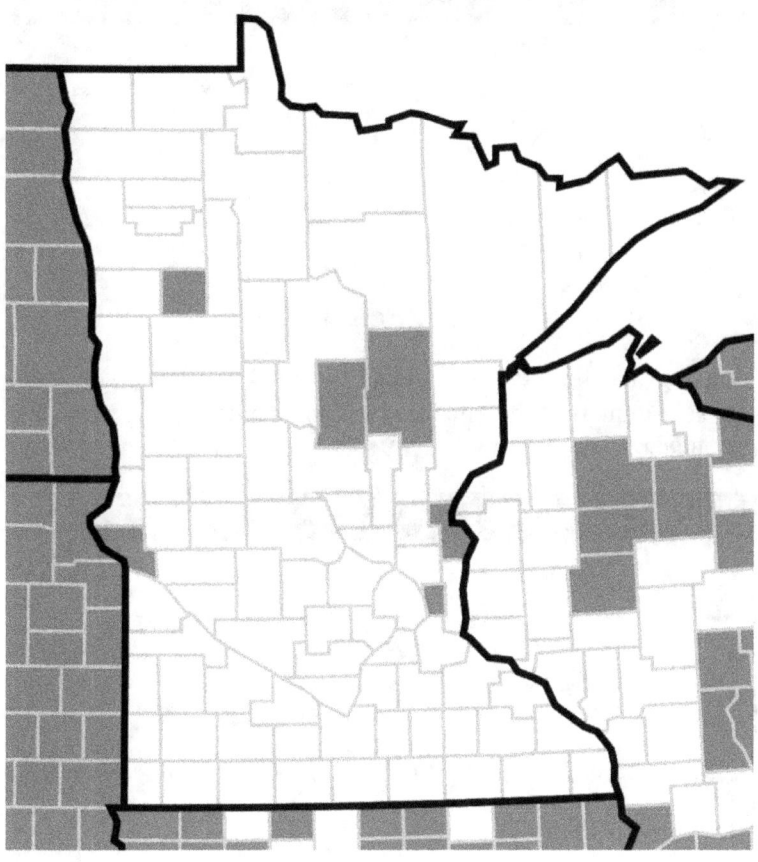

MN EAC Certification Map

Here are the counties in Minnesota that were certified by the EAC as of April 2022:

Chapter Nine - A Brief History of Voting Machines and Certifications

State	County	Manufacturer	Product	Version
Minnesota	Big Stone County	Hart	Verity	2.2
Minnesota	Chisago County	Hart	Verity	2.2
Minnesota	Ramsey County	Hart	Verity	2.2
Minnesota	Aitkin County	Dominion	D-Suite	4.14-E
Minnesota	Crow Wing County	Dominion	D-Suite	4.14-E
Minnesota	Mahnomen County	Dominion	D-Suite	4.14-E

County EAC Certifications

Thinking that this felt off, I called the EAC and left a voicemail and sent a question by email, which was replied to the same day (04/20/2022).

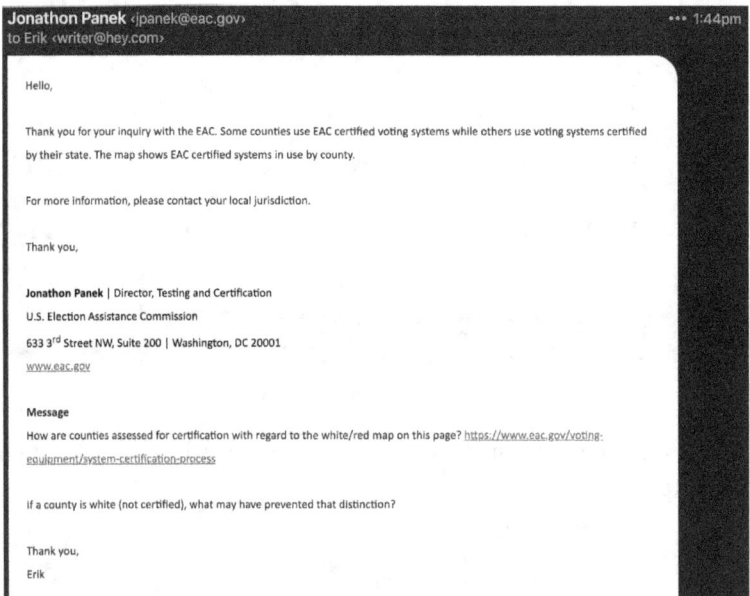

EAC email reply

This may have been comforting if not for a close reading of Minnesota election law.

Minnesota Statute 206.57, Subd.6[209] states in full:

Subd. 6.Required certification.

In addition to the requirements in subdivision 1, a voting system must be certified by an independent testing authority accredited by the Election Assistance Commission or appropriate federal agency responsible for testing and certification of compliance with the federal voting systems guidelines at the time of submission of the application required by subdivision 1 to be in conformity with voluntary voting system guidelines issued by the Election Assistance Commission or other previously referenced agency. The application must be accompanied by the certification report of the voting systems test laboratory. A certification under this section from an independent testing authority accredited by the Election Assistance Commission or other previously referenced agency meets the requirement of Minnesota Rules, part 8220.0350[210], item L. A vendor must provide a copy of the source code for the voting system to the secretary of state. A chair of a major political party or the secretary of state may select, in consultation with the vendor, an independent third-party evaluator to examine the source code to ensure that it functions as represented by the vendor and that the code is free from defects. A major political party that elects to have the source code examined must pay for the examination. Except as provided by this subdivision, a source code that is trade secret information must be treated as nonpublic information, according to section 13.37[211]. A third-party evaluator must not disclose the source code to anyone else.

It is important to note that as of now there are no other appropriate federal agencies outside of the Election Assistance Commission (EAC), which itself authorizes Pro V&V and SLI Compliance.

Are There Limits to Certifications from the EAC?

---

[209] https://www.revisor.mn.gov/statutes/cite/206.57
[210] https://www.revisor.mn.gov/rules/8220.0350/
[211] https://www.revisor.mn.gov/statutes/cite/13.37

Chapter Nine - A Brief History of Voting Machines and Certifications

Let's take a look at the EAC certification for Dominion 4.14-E[212].

EAC Certification for Dominion 4.14-E

United States Election Assistance Commission

Certificate of Conformance

Dominion Voting Systems
Democracy Suite 4.14-E

The voting system identified on this certificate has been evaluated at an accredited voting system testing laboratory for conformance to the 2005 *Voluntary Voting System Guidelines (2005 VVSG)*. Components evaluated for this certification are detailed in the attached Scope of Certification document. This certificate applies only to the specific version and release of the product in its evaluated configuration. The evaluation has been verified by the EAC in accordance with the provisions of the EAC *Voting System Testing* and *Certification Program Manual* and the conclusions of the testing laboratory in the test report are consistent with the evidence adduced. This certificate is not an endorsement of the product by any agency of the U.S. Government and no warranty of the product is either expressed or implied.

Product Name: Democracy Suite
Model or Version: 4.14-E
Name of VSTL: NTS Huntsville
EAC Certification Number: DVS-DemSuite4.14-E
Date Issued: 07/02/2015

Chief Operating Officer & Acting Executive Director
U.S. Election Assistance Commission

Scope of Certification Attached

On page 1[213] note the last sentence:

"This certificate is not an endorsement of the product by any agency of the U.S. Government and no warranty of the product is either expressed or implied."

On page 2 it reads:

---

[212] https://www.dropbox.com/s/b0efp9zqshzj1cm/EAC%20Report_DVS4.14E_FinalCert_FINAL_7.2.15.pdf?dl=0

[213] https://www.dropbox.com/s/b0efp9zqshzj1cm/EAC%20Report_DVS4.14E_FinalCert_FINAL_7.2.15.pdf?dl=0

Manufacturer: Dominion Voting
System Name: Democracy Suite 4.14-E
Certificate: DVS-DemSuite4.14-E

Laboratory: NTS Huntsville
Standard: VVSG 1.0 (2005)
Date: July 2, 2015

Scope of Certification

This document describes the scope of the validation and certification of the system defined above. Any use, configuration changes, revision changes, additions or subtractions from the described system are not included in this evaluation.

Significance of EAC Certification

An EAC certification is an official recognition that a voting system (in a specific configuration or configurations) has been tested to and has met an identified set of Federal voting system standards. An EAC certification is **not**:

- An endorsement of a Manufacturer, voting system, or any of the system's components.
- A Federal warranty of the voting system or any of its components.
- A determination that a voting system, when fielded, will be operated in a manner that meets all HAVA requirements.
- A substitute for State or local certification and testing.
- A determination that the system is ready for use in an election.
- A determination that any particular component of a certified system is itself certified for use outside the certified configuration.

Page 2 of EAC Certification for Dominion 4.14-E

Note the second to last bullet point in "Significance of EAC Certification":

"An EAC certification is **not**: A determination that the system is ready for use in an election."

Then what might these certifications be for?

Are they meant to give the public a false sense of security?

Finally, compare the full 14-page EAC certification[214] to the State of Minnesota Secretary of State Certification of Dominion Democracy Suite Version 4.14-E Voting System reproduced below:

---

[214] https://www.dropbox.com/s/b0efp9zqshzj1cm/EAC%20Report_DVS4.14E_FinalCert_FINAL_7.2.15.pdf?dl=0

Chapter Nine - A Brief History of Voting Machines and Certifications

State of Minnesota
SECRETARY OF STATE

Certification of Dominion Democracy Suite Version 4.14-E Voting System

I, Steve Simon, Secretary of State of Minnesota, hereby certify that:

Dominion Voting Systems (Dominion) has requested that the Office of the Minnesota Secretary of State examine and certify the Dominion Democracy Suite Version 4.14-E Voting System (D.S. 4.14-E) for use in Minnesota elections as certified to the 2005 Voluntary Voting System Guidelines, version 1.0 (2005 VVSG). This system includes the following components:

- Democracy Suite Election Management System (EMS)
- ImageCast Evolution (ICE) – precinct polling place optical scanner that incorporates a ballot marking device to accommodate accessibility needs
- ImageCast Central (ICC) – central count optical scan ballot tabulator. (Using commercial-off-the-shelf (COTS) Canon DR-G1130 Scanner)

Software:
- Election Event Designer – version 4.14.38 – EMS software
- Results Tally and Reporting – version 4.14.38 – EMS software
- File System Service – version 4.14.38 – EMS software
- Audio Studio – version 4.14.38 – EMS software
- Data Center Manager – version 4.14.38 – EMS software
- Application Server – version 4.14.38 – EMS software
- EMS Database Server – version 4.14.38
- EMS Election Data Translator (EDT) – version 4.14.38
- EMS NAS Server – version 4.14.38
- ImageCast Evolution (ICE) – version 4.14.25
- ImageCast Central (ICC) - version 4.14.17

Hardware:
- ICE – Firmware version 4.14.25; Model PCOS – 410A
- ICC – version 4.14.17
- ICE Plastic Box Model – Box-410A

COTS Software:
- Canon DR-G1130 Scanner

Page 1 of the State of Minnesota Secretary of State Certification of Dominion Democracy Suite Version 4.14-E Voting System

And page 2 of the same:

Review of the application submitted for D.S. 4.14-E indicates satisfaction of the requirements of Minnesota Rule 8220.0350. D.S. 4.14-E is a modification to the Democracy Suite version 4.14-D Voting System (D.S. 4.14-D), which is a modification to the Dominion Democracy Suite version 4.14-B Voting System (D.S. 4.14-B), which is a modification to the Dominion Democracy Suite version 4.14-A Voting System (D.S. 4.14-A), which is a modification to the Dominion Democracy Suite version 4.14 Voting System (D.S. 4.14), which is a modification to the Dominion Democracy Suite version 4.0 Voting System (D.S. 4.0), which received EAC Certification May 10, 2012. The independent test lab report of National Technical Systems (NTS) for D.S. 4.14-E, dated June 25, 2015, makes reference to the independent test lab results of NTS for D.S. 4.14-D which had been previously certified.

This certification relies on the independent test lab certification results of National Technical Systems (NTS) and Wyle Laboratories, Inc. (Wyle) regarding D.S. 4.14-E, dated June 25, 2015, Democracy Suite 4.14-D, dated November 19, 2014, Democracy Suite 4.14-B, dated December 19, 2013, Democracy Suite 4.14-A, dated September 26, 2013, Democracy Suite 4.14, dated September 12, 2013, and Democracy Suite 4.0, dated May 10, 2012. In reliance upon these independent test lab results and the results of the office of the Minnesota Secretary of State's certification testing as reported in the "Certification Report and Recommendation Dominion Democracy Suite Version 4.14-E Voting System" (Certification Report) the Democracy Suite 4.14-E Voting System of Dominion Voting Systems as measured to the 2005 VVSG complies with the requirements of Minnesota Statutes sections 206.55 to 206.90 and is hereby certified for use in Minnesota elections, subject to the ICC ambiguous mark threshold being set at 12% to 15% and the ICE ambiguous mark threshold being set at 22% to 25%.

This certification is subject to Minnesota Statutes and Rules. By operating under this certification, Dominion stipulates that it will employ methods and procedures to safeguard system software and firmware from access by unauthorized parties during all phases of election preparation, including preparation and delivery of election programming and related materials to county and local governments.

Witness my hand and the Great Seal of the State of Minnesota on this 30th day of March 2016.

Steve Simon
Secretary of State

Page 2 of the State of Minnesota Secretary of State Certification of Dominion Democracy Suite Version 4.14-E Voting System

What did you notice?

It reads very similarly, sometimes verbatim, to the EAC's certifications, which the EAC admits do not indicate a voting machine is ready for use in an election. If the secretary of state is using much of the EAC's language to describe the certification, and the EAC certificates themselves say they are not a determination of whether a system is ready for use in an election, how then did the secretary of state deem them ready for use?

Should the public have questions when 81 out of 87 counties in Minnesota DO NOT have certified election equipment according to the Election Assistance Commission, which under Minnesota Statute 206.57 Subd.6[215] those election machines should have prior to use?

Are there consequences to certifications (the EAC certifications) which have disclaimers putting the value of the certification itself into question? Should we be concerned when our secretary of state basically copy-pasted the EAC's certificate language into his own machine certifications?

Thank you for reading [S]elections in Minnesota. The digital versions, both written and audio, will remain free forever. If you enjoyed it, please share it with a friend, even a brand new friend.

Selections in Minnesota[216]

Erik for Secretary of State[217]

Erik for SOS on Telegram[218]

---

[215] https://www.revisor.mn.gov/statutes/cite/206.57
[216] https://leanpub.com/sim2020
[217] https://erikformn.us
[218] https://t.me/erikmn

Afterward

As I wrap up the writing on the paperback version in late June, 2022, we are entering a new phase.

Weapons of mass deception are failing and people are waking up to the truth. A truth for which they have long hungered.

It is said once one has seen, he cannot unsee.

That was how it was for me, with the election evidence.

But also, the grammer of "once one has seen, he cannot unsee" holds for seeking the truth: once one has tasted the truth, experienced it, then it can no longer be unknown. It can no longer be cast out of one's being.

Yes, we all may be flawed humans, carrying along our tragedies and misteps. Some of us were long lost, then found.

I follow Jesus and no one else, though I do not pretend to fully comprehend what I mean when I say that. It is just the best way so far of describing how I now live my life.

I feel deep within that there is so much yet to learn. About where I come from. About what we are doing here. About what we are capable of.

As that learning goes on, my soul will patiently endure the present trials and with active persistence run the race put before me.

—Erik van Mechelen, June 26, 2022

www.ingramcontent.com/pod-product-compliance
Lightning Source LLC
LaVergne TN
LVHW010318070526
838199LV00065B/5598